970439

AN INQUIRY INTO PHYSIOCRACY

AN INQUIRY INTO
PHYSIOCRACY

M. Beer

Ex natura ius, ordo, et leges,
Ex homine arbitrium, regimen,
et coercitio.

FRANCOIS QUESNAY

NEW YORK

RUSSELL & RUSSELL · INC

1966

FIRST PUBLISHED IN 1939
BY GEORGE ALLEN & UNWIN LTD.

REISSUED, 1966, BY RUSSELL & RUSSELL, INC.
BY ARRANGEMENT WITH FRANK CASS & CO. LTD., LONDON
L.C. CATALOG CARD NO: 66-15949

Printed in Great Britain

INTRODUCTION

THE present book, though its subject-matter forms a part of French pre-revolutionary thought, is, doctrinally, a sequel to my *Early British Economics* (1938). The two volumes are complementary to one another. The various medieval and early modern conceptions of trade and commerce are in the present volume more sharply defined, and general economic problems are here treated with greater sureness than in the former. The reading and re-reading of Boisguillebert and Quesnay, opposed as they are to mercantilist teaching and in sympathy with medieval ethics, assisted me in arriving at a more intimate understanding of the periods in question. On the other hand, my *Early British Economics* is richer in material, and is therefore often referred to in the present volume.

In view of the large number of books that have been published on every important problem or phase of economic theory and life, it is surprising to notice that so little has been written by British and American economic historians on the subject of physiocracy. Apart from H. Higgs's *The Physiocrats* (1897), there exists in English no separate treatise on the subject. His book contains six lectures, sketching in an instructive manner the literary history and views of François Quesnay and his followers, but it does not go materially beyond Adam Smith's treatment of the "agricultural system" or the "Economists" (*Wealth of*

Nations, book iv, chap. 9). French economic literature dealing with physiocracy is far richer; there are several large monographs on Quesnay and his School, as well as histories of the movement as a whole. None of them, however, contains more substance than Adam Smith's above-mentioned chapter.

Our knowledge of physiocracy, then, is still confined to the view that the adherents of that doctrine looked upon agriculture as the only source of wealth, and upon arts and crafts and manufacture as unproductive (sterile) occupations; further, that Quesnay composed a *Tableau Économique* which, on account of its obscurities, has vexed many a keen intellect. We are thus still in the dark as to how and why the physiocrats, men of great knowledge, wide experience of life, and lucidity of thought, could hold such views and defend them against all the arguments and obvious facts adduced by their opponents. We ought not to forget that among the creators and adherents of that school of political economy there were men, such as Quesnay, whom Adam Smith revered as a profound thinker, and Turgot, a statesman of historic importance, to mention only those two.

What, then, is the meaning of physiocracy? What were its doctrinal sources and the causes of its rise? What was its aim and end?

It is with these questions that the following pages will deal, and to which they will attempt to suggest an answer. The present book is of small size, all secondary matter and non-essential factors and details having been rigorously removed. It could have been increased to double the number of pages with hardly more than some physical effort. The increase in length would, however, only have enhanced the published price of the book, but by no means its theoretical value. As it is, the little volume will take, I believe, longer in reading than many a big book.

The author regards it as one of his most pleasant duties to thank Professor R. H. Tawney for having gone through the typescript; further Dr. James Bonar, Dr. Rosenstein Rodan, and the librarian of University College, London, for having lent him Quesnay's *Œuvres*, Dupont's *La Physiocratie* (the latter from the library and with the autograph of Jeremy Bentham), Le Mercier de la Rivière's *L'Ordre naturel et essentiel*, and G. Schelle's *Dupont de Nemours*.

Dr. Bonar, in lending me the latter book, wrote to me (September 23, 1938): "You have an excellent subject, and I believe you will make a much better book on it than Schelle. May I live to read it." These words of the aged scholar and author of *Philosophy and Political Economy* have been a great encouragement to me to do my best and to come up to his expectations. He is now eighty-eight years of age, and I passed the seventy-fifth anniversary of my birthday in August last, on which day I wrote the final chapter of the present book.

M. BEER

LONDON
September 23, 1939

CONTENTS

I

PHYSIOCRACY AS A PROBLEM

1. *Preliminary Remarks*

The French School of Economists, known also since 1767 as Physiocracy, arose from two causes—one economic and the other ethical. In the minds of its adherents the two causes were fused into a doctrine which imparted to their reasonings a high degree of social fervour. Physiocracy was a reaction from Mercantilism,[1] with its promotion of manufacture and traffic, its discriminating tariffs and balance of trade policy, or, sociologically speaking, a reaction from the industrial revolution which was set on foot in France in the seventeenth century.

The leading minds of the School, with François Quesnay at the head, were striving, as it seems, for a return to the pre-industrial era. They generalized their views in the economic doctrine that agriculture was the

[1] The characteristics of mercantilism are: (i) Conception of money (coin and bullion or treasure) as the essence of wealth. (This conception prevailed from the end of the Middle Ages up to the end of the seventeenth century.) (ii) Regulating foreign trade with a view to bringing in money by the balance of trade. (iii) Making the balance of trade the criterion of national prosperity or decline. (iv) Promotion of manufacture by supplying it with cheap raw materials and cheap labour. (v) Protective customs duties on, or prohibition of, import of manufactured commodities. (vi) The view that the economic interests of nations are mutually antagonistic.

only source of riches or the only productive occupation, while manufacture and traffic were sterile. They appeared to be the representatives of the landed interests, and were particularly opposed to the mercantilist policy as applied by J. B. Colbert in the first half of the reign of Louis XIV (1660–1683) and continued by his successors.

The inordinate fostering of "sterile" manufacture at the expense of productive tillage; the striving for a monetary balance of trade; the restrictive regulations imposed on trade and commerce, and, finally, the age-long restrictions on the marketing and exportation of grain, formed, as the physiocrats maintained,[1] the source of the misery of the French people, and were the cause of all social distempers and devastating wars between nations. They believed that those policies and restrictions, mainly due to mercantilism, were in conflict with the moral basis of economic life, that is, with equality of exchanges, just prices, or commutative justice,[2] which ought to govern the commercial trans-

[1] Until towards the end of the eighteenth century they were mainly known as "economists"; later on the appellation "physiocrats" came into general use.

[2] Justice, according to Aristotle and the Schoolmen, is twofold —distributive and commutative. The former consists in the rights and duties, the benefits and charges, apportioned by authority to the various orders and citizens, according to their station. Distributive Justice thus implies inequality of the component parts of society, but each receiving what is due to it according to its services: *sum cuique*. On the other hand, commutative justice is based on equality. It concerns the exchange of commodities or dealings between buyer and seller, and it demands that the exchange should be reciprocal and equal, value for value, without loss to one or gain to the other, but to the mutual

actions between man and man, between province and province, between nation and nation, without regard to the political frontiers which separated them from one another.

The physiocrats, universalist in religion and pre-industrial in their economic outlook, were necessarily averse from nationalist mercantilism. They believed that they had found the effective remedies: (i) economically, in the return to tillage as the principal occupation of the people; (ii) ethically, in restoring natural justice and liberty by abrogating all governmental enactments that interfered with commercial intercourse, or in allowing nature to rule (*physei-kratia*—nature's rule) according to its inherent laws given to it by Providence. Man-made laws are but injurious, for "le monde va de lui-même."[1]

Physiocracy would thus appear to be a system of advanced liberalism or a foundation for a constitution of a peasant democracy. So, indeed, it appeared to some French historians, who regarded the physiocrats as precursors of the French Revolution.[2] Yet the same school held absolute royal authority (*despotisme légal*, *autorité tutélaire*) as the best form of government, and advocated the total exclusion of all the three orders

benefit of both (St. Thomas Aquinas, *Summa*, *Secunda Secundae*, questio 61, articulus 1 and 2.

[1] Le Mercier de la Rivière, *L'Ordre naturel et essentiel*, ed. 1910, p. 338 (hereinafter referred to as Le Mercier).

[2] Alexis de Tocqueville, *L'Ancien Régime et la Révolution*, Paris, 1856, pp. 242–243. He writes of the physiocrats: "Ils ont déja conçu la pensée de toutes les réformes sociales et administratives que la Révolution a faites."

of society—nobility, merchants and manufacturers, the peasantry and the labouring population—from participation in political matters. It extolled unrestricted competition in all commercial dealings and exchanges, and at the same time it refused liberty to money-lending, and advocated governmental fixing of the rate of interest. It regarded commerce as necessary and beneficial, and at the same time as a financial burden upon the people; none the less, it exempted the merchant from all taxation. In the midst of the industrial revolution which opened up new and abundant sources of wealth, the physiocrats tenaciously maintained that manufacture was sterile. The school worked for the free exportation of all produce, and yet they regarded foreign trade or traffic as a *pis-aller*, a necessary evil. Finally, physiocracy glorified tillage as the only productive work, and yet it assigned the *produit net*, the net income or the profit of tillage, not to the cultivators as reward of their labour, but as a tribute to be paid to the landlords.

Physiocracy, then, as its main characteristics would show, presents itself as a compound of inconsistent views and contradictory tenets, yoking together most modern and strictly medieval doctrines. And yet it cannot be denied that physiocratic thought was elaborated with much knowledge and defended with logical acumen by its authors. We may, indeed, apply to physiocracy the characteristic saying of Victor Hugo on the elder Mirabeau (the friend of Quesnay and his premier interpreter): "un très rare penseur, qui est à la fois en arrière et en avant de son temps."[1] It undoubtedly influenced the course of political economy. The School had also two precursors bearing great names—Fénelon and Boisguillebert.

In short, physiocracy forms a problem in the history of economics, on the merits and implications of which the most divergent opinions have been current.

Loménie, in one of the most informative and vivacious volumes on the Mirabeau family, deals also with physiocracy and makes the remark that there is something strange about that School. It occurs often enough that a new doctrine gives rise to a good deal of disagreement among its contemporaries about its meaning and value. What, however, is less comprehensible is that physiocracy, though long since defunct and having left nothing behind but a few printed books, should still form the subject of the most various interpretations by nineteenth-century writers, such as Tocqueville, Daire, Louis Blanc, Proudhon, Taine, Lavergne, etc. In support of his statement, Loménié fills several pages of his book with quotations, the gist of which is that the physiocrats were regarded by some as revolutionists and levellers, by others as bourgeois reformers and *laissez-faire* liberals, finally as reactionaries and feudal utopians.[2]

Henry Higgs, evidently following Loménie, opens his first lecture on the physiocrats with the words: "The physiocrats have been the subject of so many

[1] Loménie, *Les Mirabeau*, Paris, 1879–1891, vol. ii, p. 1.
[2] *Ibid.*, pp. 175–182.

and such divergent appreciation by historians, philosophers, economists, and students of political science that hardly a single general proposition of importance has been advanced with regard to them by one writer which has not been contradicted by another." He then refers to the above-mentioned writers, adding to them Thomas Carlyle and Professor Gustav Cohn, who likewise differ in their opinion of physiocracy.[1]

To an Englishman physiocracy might well seem to be a hybrid product of Toryism and "Cobdenism." And he would not be far from the truth. In the latter half of the seventeenth century similar notions were germinating in England, but failed to develop to the same extent as physiocratic ideas a century later in France. They only gave us several ardent Tories with free-trade aspirations and theories, the most outstanding names among them being Sir Josiah Child, Sir Dudley North, and Sir Charles Davenant. No valid explanation has yet been given of the rise of the "Tory Free Trade," to which Sir William Ashley has directed the attention of economic students.[2] What causes were operating that called forth free trade ideas among Tories after the Civil War?

A systematic inquiry into the circumstances of the rise of physiocracy and, in a lesser degree, of the rise of Tory free trade, may perhaps lead us to a solution of the problem.

[1] H. Higgs, *The Physiocrats*, 1897, pp. 1–2.
[2] Sir William Ashley, *Surveys*, London, 1900, p. 268, *passim*.

2. *The Corn Trade in England*

Foreign trade in merchandise was in the Middle Ages
free from prohibitions and protective duties. Only in
times of war was the export of certain merchandise
temporarily prohibited to distress the enemy. It was
in all Christian countries acknowledged that God
endowed the various regions of the earth with different
climates and produce for the purpose of inducing men
to exchange their goods with one another and thus to
promote amity and peaceful intercourse among mankind.[1] Foreign trade was in principle free, subject only
to customs duties, impositions, etc., to supply the
revenue of the Crown with coin and bullion. The
regulations concerning foreign trade had, as a
rule, no direct reference to the promotion or protection of native trade. They were mainly fiscal or
ethical.

The only prohibitive laws or ordinances concerned
the exportation of coin (bullion) and corn, since coin
and foodstuffs were not primarily regarded as merchandise. The valuation and exchange of coin were
royal prerogatives, and were exercised through the
monetarius regis.[2] Exportation of coin and bullion could
only be effected by royal licence. Numerous are the
ordinances prohibiting the carrying away of money.
Even as late as the first quarter of the seventeenth

[1] See, for instance, John Gower, *Mirour de l'Omme*, lines
25177–25185. For other references see the author's *Early British
Economics*, pp. 57–58.

[2] *Early British Economics*, pp. 63–64.

century, some writers condemned the "merchandising" of "exchanges."[1] As to corn, the evidence is likewise clear. In the Statutes of the Realm and in economic writings of early modern times we find generally the phrase "merchandise and victuals." Corn and fish were known as victuals and not as merchandise. They were, above all, esteemed as food, the marketing of which was regulated with a view (i) to bring producer and consumer together; (ii) to secure for both a just price; (iii) to restrict the movements of the corn-mongers, so as to prevent speculation in victuals. The farmer was to bring his produce to the market appointed for that purpose. It was illegal to "forestall"—that is, to buy victuals "on their way to the market or port, or contracting to buy the same before actually brought for sale, or endeavouring to enhance the price or prevent supply" reaching the market. It was illegal to "regrate," that is, to buy victuals for business purposes and to "sell them in the same place or within four miles thereof." It was illegal to "engross," that is, to buy up corn when it is still growing or to "corner" it for the purpose of selling it later when it is dear (*Statutes of the Realm*, 5 & 6 Edw. VI, chap. 14). Those were the statutes regulating the internal corn trade in England till 1663.

As to exportation of corn, it may be said that in Norman and Angevin times the exportation was, as a rule, prohibited, and importation of corn permitted. Exportation was only by special royal licence. The

---

[1] *Early British Economics*, pp. 110–111.

Carta Mercatoria (1303) granted to alien merchants general licence to export corn, but this privilege was later revoked. In 1393 Richard II, at the request of the Commons, granted licence "to all his liege people" to carry corn out of the realm, "paying subsidies and *devoirs*." The King's Council had, however, the right to restrain the exportation, if they should think it for the benefit of the Realm (*Statutes of the Realm*, 17 Richard II, chap. 7). The traditional views were indeed strong enough to induce the King's Council to obstruct the exportation of corn. Still, during the greater part of the fifteenth century some corn was exported from the sea-coast counties by virtue of the said statute. In 1463 King Edward IV prohibited the importation of corn, owing to the abnormally low prices which ruled in the home market. This Statute (3 Edw. IV, chap. 2) was the first protective corn law, but it had to wait for a sequel until 1670.

With the accession of Henry VII the statutory facilities for corn exportation gradually ceased, and corn importation was permitted. Henry VIII followed the same policy, but in the reign of Elizabeth a change of export policy took place. The legislation concerning export of victuals was guided by two considerations— promotion of navigation and the price-level of corn. Besides permitting in 1562 (5 Eliz., chap. 5) the free exportation of fish in English-built ships, the Queen, in 1571 (13 Eliz., chap. 13), granted free exportation of corn in English ships if the price of wheat did not exceed 20s. per quarter. As to the home corn trade, the

Queen followed the very strict regulations of 5 & 6 Edw. VI, chap. 14, quoted above.

The Stuarts followed the Elizabethan corn legislation. The Commonwealth likewise, but as regards wool, one of its first laws (1649) prohibited the exportation of wool, the most important English staple commodity in the European cloth manufacture in medieval and early modern times. It lowered considerably the price of wool in the home market to the benefit of the native manufacturers and to the injury of the landed interests.

To sum up: since the end of the fourteenth century the landed interests demanded the abrogation of the restrictions which had been imposed by statute and tradition on the exportation of agricultural produce. We shall see in a later chapter how that demand led to the formulation of physiocratic and free trade views by Tory writers.

3. *The Corn Trade in France*

In France the restrictions on the home trade of corn, which were formulated in royal edicts or ordinances, continued a hundred years longer than in England, that is, to 1764,[1] though free trade in corn

---

[1] The abrogation of the restrictive laws was one of the short-lived successes of the physiocratic school. The Edict in question declares that its purpose is to promote the extension of agriculture, the produce of which is "la source la plus réelle et la plus sûre des richesses d'un État . . ." and to allow free competition to operate in commerce; finally, to maintain between nations the

lasted only for a brief period. The Church, the Schoolmen, the Canonists, and generally medieval conceptions, had there a stronger vitality, a more vigorous
hold on the authorities and the people than in England,
where the Reformation gradually undermined and
partly obliterated medievalist traditions and views.
Neither Calvin, the anti-Catholic theologian, nor
Descartes, the anti-scholastic philosopher, could find
a home in their native country. Schoolmen's views on
trade and commerce are even to be met with in French
social reform writings in the middle of the nineteenth
century.[1] French socialism from the times of Babeuf
(1793) to Proudhon (1848) is largely based either on
ius naturale or on interpretations of the Gospel and
Fathers.

It may be stated as a rule that royal edicts, ordi-

exchange of their surplus for necessaries "et conforme à l'ordre
établi par la divine Providence et aux vues d'humanité qui doivent
animer tous les souverains" (quoted in Depitre's edition of Le
Mercier, *L'Ordre naturel*, Paris, 1910, p. x). See also Adam Smith,
Wealth of Nations, book iv, chap. 9.

[1] Readers who are interested in the history of Socialist theory
will probably find the following remark suggestive: The whole
controversy between Proudhon and Marx in the years 1844–1850
was inevitable. Proudhon's starting-point was the problem, how
to create a society which should be based on commutative justice,
on equal exchanges to the mutual benefit of producer and consumer; Proudhon's inquiry into value had that purpose in view
(*mutualisme*). Marx's starting-point was the problem, under what
economic and, generally, social conditions would the proletariat
rise and create a communist society; Marx's inquiry into value
had for its purpose to demonstrate that the surplus value wrested
from the proletariat by Capital must eventually lead to crisis, class
warfare, and revolution. Proudhon's sources were the Schoolmen;
Marx's sources the revolutionary writers (such as Aug. Blanqui)
and his own interpretation of Hegel and Ricardo.

nances, and even statutes of the realm, which are transmitted to us from the Middle Ages or early modern times, are no safe guides to our knowledge of the practice which they were supposed to introduce or to regulate. Comparatively few people read them, and very often the local authorities or local influences obstructed them. There was no bureaucracy and no police, such as we know now, to enforce the statutes and watch over their execution. Only those edicts and statutes are safe guides for which there exists well-established evidence that they were carried into effect. This applies to France as well as England.[1]

As to the exportation of corn, it is generally acknowledged that during the sixteenth century there was no fixed policy. It all depended on the quantity and quality of the harvest. Exportation of grain was alternately permitted or prohibited according to the abundance and scarcity of victuals in the local markets.

The accession of Henry IV in 1589 brought, at first, no decisive change in that respect. His reputation as a friend of agriculture is well founded only as regards his care for improvements in tillage, draining of marshes, protection against marauding bands, curbing the arbitrariness of the landed noblemen in

[1] Thorold Rogers writes (Palgrave's *Dictionary of Political Economy*, vol. i, p. 424, art. "Corn Laws"): "For a very long time Acts of Parliament were very imperfectly obeyed, perhaps hardly known to exist." As to royal edicts in France, Montchrétien declares: "Les Édictes de France sont ordinairement meilleur que bien observées" (*Traicté de l'Œconomie Politique* (1615), ed. Funck-Brentano, p. 248. See also Lavisse, *Histoire de France*, vol. vi, part 2, p. 73).

their dealing with the tenants, reducing the rate of interest, greater willingness to permit, as far as he could, the exportation of corn, for, as he declared in an edict of 1595, the opening of the foreign market would enable the peasantry to obtain better prices and to attract silver from the foreigner, "en quoi ils doivent principalement viser." A larger measure of freedom of the corn trade was granted to all the provinces by an edict of 1601. Exportation appears to have been henceforth generally permitted, while prohibitions were exceptions.

French agriculture was at that time regarded as the main source of wealth and as a means to obtain treasure from abroad, while manufacture was considered only as a means to retain the treasure in the country by giving the consumer the opportunity to buy native manufactured commodities. This was also the principle of Sully's administration. He declared: "Le patûrage et le labourage sont les deux mamelles dont la France est alimentée, ses vraies mines et trésors de Perou. . . . C'est par l'exportation de nos produits agricoles . . . que nous pouvons faire entrer en France le numéraire étranger. C'est en encourageant les industries . . . que nous pouvons l'empêcher d'en sortir."[1]

Though we do not know for certain how the edicts of 1601 worked in practice, we may assume that the corn trade enjoyed greater freedom than formerly. In

[1] Lavisse, *Histoire de France*, vol. vi, part 2, p. 70; Pigeonneau, *Histoire du Commerce*, vol. ii, pp. 250–280.

the memory of the agricultural population the reign of Henry IV continued to live as the golden age of tillage. The physiocrats always refer to Henry IV and Sully as the Romans used to refer to the reign of Saturn, when justice ruled on earth. Boisguillebert and Quesnay, who are full of praise of Henry IV and Sully and severely censorious of Colbert, forget, however, that the rise of French mercantilism began in the reign of Henry IV and that it was one of his ministers, namely, Barthélemy de Laffemas, who formulated it.[1]

[1] On the English and French corn trade, see Charles Davenant, *Works*, vol. v, p. 424; Ch. Smith, *Corn Trade Tracts*, ed. 1804, pp. 29, 38, 74; W. Cunningham, *Growth of English Industry*, vol. i; R. Faber, *Entstehung des Agrarschutzes in England*, 1888; W. Naudé, *Getreide-Handel*, 1892; A. P. Usher, *History of the Grain Trade in France*, 1913; N. S. B. Gras, *Evolution of the Corn Trade*, 1915.

II

FRENCH MERCANTILISM

1. *Economic Conditions in the Sixteenth Century*

The influx of treasure from Spain since the third decade of the sixteenth century brought a rising market to French agriculture, arts and crafts, and the few industries, mainly linen, silks, and inferior cloth, which were being established in various parts of the country. In the second half of the century, France became the purveyor of Spain in grain, linen, pastel, paper, books, some woollens, and all sorts of household wares. Moreover, most of the craftsmen employed in Spain were French, and they brought back their savings in Spanish currency. The foreign trade was, however, mostly in the hands of alien merchants.

As everywhere in the Middle Ages, free trade in merchandise was also the rule in France, that is, there were, in peace times, no prohibitions, but various customs duties for fiscal purposes, which were not regarded as an infringement of freedom of commerce. In the second half of the sixteenth century, however, influential men—*grands personnages*, as Jean Bodin calls them—demanded restrictions on foreign trade, which Bodin combats in the traditional, medieval way by pointing out that God endowed the various regions of the earth with different climates and produce, so that men should be obliged to exchange their goods, supply each other's deficiencies, and thus to promote amity and friendship among mankind. Even if we could do without exchanges with strangers it would still be necessary to "trafiquer, vendre, acheter, échanger, prêter, voire plûtot donner une partie de nos biens aux étrangers." It is our national duty not to withhold God's gifts from others. Therefore, he declares, he could not agree to prohibitions, except for moral reasons, of certain Italian imports, such as female attire, perfumes, false diamonds, and poisons. Bodin includes in these objectionable commodities also Italian "parchments," probably immoral books, such as some writers of the Renaissance produced. On the other hand, Bodin had no objection to the imposition of high export duties on French grain, wine, and salt, for the sake of obtaining silver from the foreign merchants who carried these goods away.[1]

From the statements of Bodin and the general economic condition of France in the second half of the sixteenth century, it may be inferred that France would have developed on parallel economic lines with England but for the religious and civil unrest, commotions, and massacres, which afflicted France for about a quarter century—1570 to 1595. Internal disorders devastated much of her agriculture, and paralysed her trade and commerce, so that in the first years of the reign of Henry IV she had to start her economic life

[1] *Réponse de Jean Bodin* (1568), ed. Hauser, 1932, pp. 12–16, 34–37.

anew. It is of historical significance that this constructive work was initiated by four Huguenots: Henry IV, Sully (finances), Olivier de Serres (agriculture), and Barthélemy Laffemas (commerce and manufactures). It was the latter who in the years 1596 to 1604 enunciated mercantilist principles. He was followed by Anthony Montchrétien, who, though apparently a Roman Catholic, fought and died for the Huguenots. Manufacture and mercantilism must have appeared to French Catholics as mainly the work of Protestants, that is, heretics.[1]

2. *Laffemas and the Council of Commerce*

Barthélemy (de) Laffemas, born *circa* 1545 at Beausemblant (Dauphiné), flourished as pioneer of French mercantilism in the years from 1596 to 1604. He was the son of a Protestant family belonging to the lesser nobility, but owing to the impoverishment of his parents, he learned the tailoring trade and found employment as tailor and valet in the house of Prince Henry of Navarre, later Henry IV. He followed his master to Paris and remained attached to him through all the vicissitudes which marked the life of this truly great king.

[1] Such views seem to have prevailed in the German Rhineland. Georg Forster, a well-known German traveller and writer, relates of the sister-towns Aachen (Aix la Chapelle) and Burscheid that the former (mainly inhabited by Catholics, "who oppressed and hated the Protestants") had no factories, while Burscheid, where the Protestants lived, had "big cloth and needle factories" (*Briefe und Tagebücher*, 1790, ed. 1893, pp. 17, 139).

Apart from his employment as king's tailor and valet, Laffemas was also entrusted with purchasing silver plate for the king, and according to some sources he established himself as cloth and silk merchant in Paris and acquired considerable wealth. His commercial career brought him daily into contact with the many economic difficulties that confronted France after the restoration of religious peace, and he sought for remedies and reforms. Nationally minded, as the good Protestant he was, and imbued with the business spirit of early modern times, he thought to have found the source of economic evil in the fatal dependence of France on foreign manufactures, which drained the country of its coin and bullion, the life-blood of trade and commerce.[1] He therefore adopted economic nationalism, that is, mercantilism: prohibition of import of all sorts of woollen and silk manufactures: subsidies for the establishment of home

[1] Towards the end of the sixteenth century he submitted to King Henry IV a mercantilist manifesto (*Règlement Général*) and prefaced it with the following letter:

"Sire,—Ayant eu cest honneur que d'estre vostre domestique depuis trente ans, et vous ayant fait service en mon estat de tailleur et varlet de chambre, et depuis marchant en vostre argenterie, la longuer du temps et le trafiq que j'ay fait avec plusieurs marchans estrangers, m'a fait avoir l'éxpérience pour cognoistre le mal secret et caché qu'aporte en vostre Estat les draps de soye, toilles d'or et d'argent et autres marchandises venant des pays d'Italie, de Flandres, Angleterre et autres lieux. . . ." He then continues to declare that if those abuses could be stopped, France would fulfil what seems to be God's design to make this country have "auctorité et commandement sur tous les autres" (*Collections de meilleurs notices et traités*, ed. J. M. C. Leber, Paris, 1826–1838, vol. xix, pp. 528 *et seq.*).

manufactures: prohibition of export of native raw materials, removal of all obstacles which hinder the free circulation of goods within the national boundaries.

In 1596 Laffemas addressed the Assembly of Notables in Rouen on those commercial problems, and from that year onwards he displayed great energy in disseminating his views and in attempting to introduce or develop the silkworm culture, to establish silk and woollen manufactories, glass works, metallurgy, and to improve internal communication by constructing roads and waterways, joining the Seine and Loire, and, in the south-west of France, the Mediterranean with the Atlantic. In 1601 the king appointed a commission on trade, which soon turned into a Council of Commerce, holding weekly meetings till the year 1604. The leading spirit of the Council was Laffemas. The proceedings of this Commission or Council of Commerce appear to have exercised considerable influence on Colbert.[1] In 1602 Laffemas was appointed Controller General of Commerce and Manufacture, and two years later (1604) he was able to submit to the king a full report of his plans, of the works begun, and of the industrial projects to be taken in hand.

Laffemas regarded it as necessary to develop the silkworm culture, to plant mulberry trees, and to manufacture all sorts of silks "for which at present we send abroad annually more than six million *écus*,

[1] "The papers of the Council of Commerce form part of the collection of manuscripts at the Bibliothèque Nationale (Paris) coming from the library of Colbert" (A. P. Usher, *Grain Trade in France*, p. 353).

without any substantial return, except musk, perfumes, and vanities (*objets de luxe*) which are poisoning body and soul." There were already established silk factories in Paris, Orleans, Tours, and Lyon; fine Bologna crapes at Mante, likewise gold and silver thread in Milan fashion; tapestries of gilt leather, cloth of various colours at the Faubourg Saint-Honoré and Saint-Jacques; iron foundries and steel works at Estampes; lead tubes at the Faubourg Saint-Germain. France was too much dependent on German metal wares.

As to other industries, Laffemas urged the restoration of the old glass works, which would offer employment to the impoverished lesser nobility. The old French glass works succumbed to the competition of Italian glass crystal. The Italian manufacturers in France should be compelled to indenture French apprentices and teach them the secrets of the trade. There were brought to the notice of the Commission several new inventions to be introduced: a spinning machine, which, as the inventor showed, could be tended by children and invalids, sitting at ease at their work; a process to bleach flour; production of white-lead, which was used in painting and in medicine for horses. Much French money was going to Holland for fine linen, while rich manufacturers at Rouen were ready to undertake this branch of linen industry. There were also offers from manufacturers to introduce carpet making.

English fustian, declared Laffemas, was really

worked in France, but finished in England, where the workers had got the secret of it. "Now we have obtained the secret it could be finished in France. The Commission have worked out the plans."

Finally, Laffemas deplored the decline of French manufacture during the civil commotions. "Fifty or sixty years ago Paris and other towns supplied all the cloth of France. Now the people were clothed by foreign stuff from Italy, Flanders, England, etc., for which so much of French money was leaving the country. "From the records of the Paris dyers we can see that in one year there were dyed 600,000 pieces of cloth, which is now being done only in six or eight years." There was, then, no time to be lost in the promotion of French manufactures. The Commission was quite aware of the opposition of some merchants to those plans and works, but they were real enemies of France, for they were in the pay of the foreigner. They ought to be deprived of all civic honours.[1]

After the year 1604 nothing more is heard of Laffemas; he seems to have retired to the country, where he died in 1612. His son, Isaac, an "advocat en Parlament," continued his father's work, and in 1606 addressed to the king a short outline of the French commercial history (*Histoire du Commerce*). In the

[1] Leber, *Collections* (as above); Cimber, *Archives Curieuses de l'Histoire de France*, Paris, 1830–1840, vols. ix and xiv; Funck-Brentano, Introduction to Montchrétien's *Traicté de l'Œconomie Politique*, 1881; Lavisse, *Histoire de France*, 1905, vol. vi, part 2, pp. 74–76.

covering letter "Au Roy" he speaks of his father's efforts and achievement for the welfare of King and Country.

3. Anthony Montchrétien

Less fertile in practical schemes, but more learned than Laffemas, was his younger contemporary writer, Anthony Montchrétien, author of *Traicté de l'Œconomie Politique* (1615), which he dedicated to the king (Louis XIII) and the king's mother, Mary de Medici. It addresses itself in direct speech to the king, and it is the first book on trade and commerce which uses the term "political economy." Montchrétien was born in Normandy about the year 1575 and received a good medieval education at the College of Caen. He was to all appearances a Roman Catholic, though he sided with the Huguenots and was killed in 1623 while fighting in their ranks. At an early age he wrote poetry and dramas, but he had the temperament of an adventurous swordsman; he fought duels and in 1603 killed an adversary in one of them. He escaped punishment by fleeing to England, where he turned his attention to economic questions.

He was surprised by the manufacturing and commercial activities of the English, studied particularly the manufacture of metal wares, and most probably read *A Briefe Conceipt of Inglish Policie* (1581), Malynes' *Canker of England's Commonwealth* (1601), and similar tracts and reports on exchanges, scarcity

of money, etc.,[1] besides reading in his own language
Bodin's epoch-making tract on the rise of prices.

On his return to Normandy he established a tool
workshop, producing cutlery, etc., and wrote his above-
mentioned book, containing about three hundred pages,
and written in an elevated, somewhat rhetorical style.
It must have been composed at various times and in
various moods, for it is by no means consistent in its
views on important economic concepts—the incon-
sistency arising from the clash between his medieval
sentiments and universalist ethics on the one hand,
and commercial individualism and nationalist interests
on the other. It is the latter that predominate and which
make the book into a strongly mercantilist treatise.

The *Traicté de l'Œconomie Politique* (edited with an
extensive introduction by Funck-Brentano in 1889) is
divided into four parts: (1) Manufacture, arts and
crafts, textiles and metals; (2) Foreign trade, transport
and currency; (3) Navigation, establishment of colonies; (4) Duties of the Government, defence, judiciary,
etc. The remarkable title of the book and the headings
of its four divisions, which might suggest the idea of a
systematic economic treatise, should not delude the
reader into the assumption that he has to do with a
work on political economy as we understand it to-day.
It is no more than a collection of early modern and
medieval views, demands and recommendations as to
how a king could bring glory and riches to his country.
It discusses and recommends the following means:

[1] Cf. the author's *Early British Economics*, 1938, pp. 82–129.

driving out all foreign traders and merchants; prohibiting all imports of manufactured commodities; working up the native raw materials into commodities; restricting or prohibiting the export of corn, so as to have cheap food for our artisans and tradespeople, who by the work of their deft fingers bring riches to the realm; fixing of prices of all goods by royal authority. By those means the money would be kept in the country, and much money would flow into the country from foreign merchants buying French goods. His arguments in support of his policy are mainly mercantilist: Money, that is, gold and silver, were the things on which we lived and by which a country waxed in might and glory. "L'or et l'argent . . . sont deux grands et fidèles amis. Ils suppléent aux nécessités de tous hommes. Ils les honorent parmi toutes gens. . . . Trafic est le plus court moyen de s'énrichir, et par les richesses monter au comble d'honneur et d'autorité" (p. 141). This is unadulterated mercantilist doctrine. Later on he relapses into medieval thought and declares (p. 241): "Ce n'est point l'abondance d'or et d'argent, la quantité de perles et de diamants qui fait les États riches et opulents, c'est l'accordement des choses nécessaires à la vie et propres au vêtment, qui plus en a, plus on a de bien." This is in agreement with Aristotle and the Schoolmen.

Likewise in agreement with those medieval authorities is his view that "agriculture is the first and most excellent of all occupations and the foundation of all powers and riches" (pp. 40–41). And he refers to

Aristotle and Cato for support of that view. Without being conscious of any contradiction, his main effort is to look for power and riches, not to agriculture, but to manufacture, traffic, and money, that is, to mercantilist policy.

Montchrétien is well aware that commerce "estant du droit des gens, doit être égal entre égaux . . . reciproquement libre et sans restrictions de pays" (p. 219). This is medieval doctrine. But as an early modern mercantilist he adds: "Il est absolument au pouvoir du prince de la restreindre à quiy il veut," and he demands a surtax on importation and even prohibition of certain goods (p. 249). He evinces a fierce hatred of the foreign traders who resided in France and acquired riches through dealings in France. They often injured the State and always the native merchants. All the laws enacted by our kings against vagabonds ought also to apply to those foreign merchants "gens de bonne chère et de grosse dépense" (pp. 169–170, 241). He justifies his hatred by appealing to ethics: "Ce qui est étranger nous corrompt." This appears to be a reminiscence from Aquinas (*De Regimine principum*, book ii, chap. 3, where the danger of corruption through alien traffickers is emphasized).

As a reader of Bodin's tract on the rise of prices and as a student of English economic tracts, Montchrétien knows the quantity theory of money and is of opinion, though not consistently, that prices depend on the quantity of money available for commerce. If money is abundant, prices rise, and *vice versa* (pp. 240–241). "Things are dearer because of the influx of treasure from America" (p. 257). He restricts this view by declaring that "While value is *immuable* the prices fluctuate for various reasons. One would think that the author would give some definition of value and show the eternal factor or factors which according to him constituted value. But nothing of the kind is given. Instead, he thrusts all economic reasonings aside and declares that the king could order through the police that the prices of victuals and merchandise should be brought back to their former level: "C'est par la seule police . . . que peuvent retourner les vivres et les marchandises à leur premier point" (p. 257). He demands also strict observance of the statutes concerning forestalling, regrating, and engrossing. This is quite medieval. None the less, Montchrétien pleads for the recognition of gain and profit as legitimate motives of, and free competition and individual interest as the best incentives, to business enterprise.

For all his medieval reactions and theoretical inconsistencies, our author must be regarded as one of the creators of French mercantilism.

4. *J. B. Colbert and Louis XIV*

The commercial and industrial reconstruction of France on mercantilist lines, which began in the reign of Henry IV, was continued by Richelieu after 1626 and later by Mazarin. It was J. B. Colbert, however, who gave the new policy coherence, and made mercantilist principles his guiding star.

Colbert was the son of a Rheims wool merchant, and received his financial training and gathered experience at an Italian banking house in Paris. One of its clients was Cardinal Mazarin, the virtual ruler of France during the regency of Anne of Austria, the widow of Louis XIII (1642–1660). On the occasion of his banking transactions he often had to deal with Colbert, of whose abilities he conceived a high opinion, and finally recommended him to Louis XIV, who ascended the throne in 1660. Colbert was appointed comptroller-general of finances, and proved himself to be an executive officer of high integrity, inexhaustible working capacity, and great financial talents. He cleansed the revenue administration of many fraudulent officials, raised the revenue, reduced the debt, extended the marine and naval ports, built waterways and roads, founded the *Académie des Sciences*, the *Jardin des Plantes*, and supported financially the poets Corneille, Racine, and Molière. But his main care was the promotion of the old manufactures and crafts and the introduction of new ones.

His official correspondence, consisting of letters, memoranda, instructions, and observations, sent to the king or his subordinates bear ample testimony to his careful and exhaustive studies of the commercial developments of the Low Countries and England. They can be read with keen pleasure even to-day. They are State Papers of great importance, and we owe it to

Emperor Napoleon III that they were edited in seven volumes by the economist Pierre Clement in 1863–1870, who rendered them more valuable to students by his introductions and notes.

Colbert began to write his memoranda on commerce and manufactures probably for Mazarin in 1650, that is, at the age of thirty. He undoubtedly read the English tracts on mercantilist policy, whose principles he made his own. France, he writes in his *Mémoire sur le Commerce* (1664) exports annually manufactured commodities to the value of between twelve to eighteen million livres (wine, spirits, iron, ironmongery, linen, paper, silks, haberdashery, fruits). "These are our silver and gold mines." But the Dutch, with their shipping and imports of Indian textiles, spices, and luxuries deprive us of most of our gains. The treasure which we obtain for our commodities flows out to the Low Countries. This must be prevented, for "il n'y a que l'abondance d'argent dans un État qui fasse la difference de sa grandeur et de sa puissance. . . . Augmenter l'argent dans le commerce public en l'attirant des pays d'ou il vient en le conservant au dedans et empêchant qu'il n'en sort et donnant des moyens aux hommes d'en tirer profit."[1] Commerce and manufacture and an appropriate fiscal and protective policy would produce that result.

From 1667 onwards he fought the Dutch, and also the English, by high tariffs. The customs duties were

[1] J. C. Colbert, *Lettres, Instructions*, etc., vol. ii, pp. cclvii, cclxx; vol. vii, pp. 233–260.

arranged according to mercantilist rules, i.e. high import duties on manufactured goods, low export duties on home-manufactured commodities, low import duties on raw materials, regulation of foreign commerce in such a manner as to procure a favourable balance of trade and to enrich the country by bringing in treasure from abroad.

Colbert's efforts to make France a great manufacturing and commercial nation, rivalling England and Holland, were crowned with much success. France knew in Colbert's times no scarcity of money; and as a manufacturing and commercial State she was reckoned to be the most formidable competitor of the English, forcing out of them millions of pounds sterling by the annual balance of trade. In English mercantilist and political writings of the period, France took the place of Holland.[1] The old enmity of England towards the Dutch, which was exceedingly bitter in the first half of the seventeenth century, receded, and that towards France grew to be one of the dominant influences on English economic policy. It led in 1678 to the total prohibition of French goods, and finally to

[1] S. Fortrey, *England's Interest and Improvement* (1673) (in McCulloch's *Select English Tracts* (1856)), pp. 232–234, states that French exports to England amounted annually to above £2,000,000, and English exports to France to only £1,000,000. Fortrey is quoted in *Britannia Languens* (1680), *ibid.*, pp. 423–424. The number and variety of French manufactured commodities enumerated by Fortrey are very considerable. I may also refer to Funck-Brentano's opinion on this matter: "À la mort de Colbert, la France était devenue, de pays agricole, pays industriel" (Introduction to Montchrétien, *Traicté de l'Œconomie Politique*, p. ci).

more than a hundred years of mutual distrust, conflicts of policy, and European and Colonial wars, which only ended with Waterloo.

Colbert's twenty-three years of ardent work for the manufacturing and commercial strength of France—1661 to 1683—which formed about the first half of Louis XIV's reign, were in economic, military, and literary respects the real glory of the age of *le roi-soleil* But there were also deep shadows, which darkened more and more in the latter half of the king's reign.

Absorbed in his practical mercantilism, Colbert left the home corn market to its traditional regulations, and with regard to corn export he returned to the pre-Sully policy, permitting or restraining exportation according to the abundance or scarcity of foodstuffs. Colbert regarded the supply of cheap food to the working people as more important than the foreign trade in corn. Formerly the corn export had aimed at getting treasure from abroad. This function it could no more fulfil. French agriculture, prosperous in the reign of Henry IV and Louis XIII, declined during the regency (1642–1660). Mazarin burdened tillage with heavy impositions; the *taille*, essentially a tax on the farming population, rose from sixteen million livres to fifty-seven millions in 1659. The *gabelle* (salt tax) and the *aides* (excise duties on wine) rose proportionately. The *Fronde*, the rebellion against Mazarin's arbitrary taxation, was crushed, but the disastrous effects of his policy persisted. Tillage was neglected, so that the first two years of the reign of Louis XIV were years of famine. These conditions might have suggested to Colbert the idea that agriculture was no more the main source of wealth and must be subordinated to the needs of manufacture as the more appropriate means to enriching the nation. In order to compensate agriculture for the injury that resulted from the restrictions, he made a serious attempt to ease the burden of taxation which pressed heavily on the tillers of the soil. The king's warlike policy, and the pomp and pageantry of the Court at Versailles, were making, however, exorbitant demands on the taxable capacity of the nation. In the first years of his reign the king gave ear to Colbert's complaints about the wasteful expenditure of the Court. In a long *Mémoire au roi,* dated July 22, 1666, Colbert writes: "Je déclare à Vôtre Majésté qu'un repas inutile de mille écus me fait une peine incroyable."[1] Later on all the admonitions of Colbert were in vain. The needs of the army and the Court had to be supplied.

The long and costly wars against Holland (1667–1687), and the prodigality of the Court, not only absorbed the rich treasure that Colbert's policy of the balance of trade brought to France, but also much of the wealth produced in field and vineyard.

In those circumstances it was impossible for Colbert thoroughly to reform the *taille* and the oppressively high *aides*. The income of the farmers—so Boisguillebert and Quesnay tell us—often fell short of the prime

---

[1] *Lettres, Instructions, Mémoires de Colbert* (edited by P. Clement, Paris, 1860–1870), vol. ii, p. cxi.

cost of production plus the amount of taxation. A whole army of tax-farmers, with their agents and parasites, battened on the labours of the husbandmen, of whose tax payment only about a third reached the royal exchequer. Quesnay, quoting Boisguillebert's *Détail de la France* (1695), writes that "in the reign of Louis XIV, the revenue amounted to over 750 millions livres, but only 250 millions were received by the exchequer."[1]

The farmer and the wine-grower were thus deprived of the incentive to work their lands for any larger output than that which would just suffice to supply their own needs. In the course of years, and progressively so after the death of Colbert (1683), much of the acreage was going out of cultivation, and many of the best vineyards were being abandoned. Wine production declined, likewise the manufacture of spirits and liqueurs. Thus some of the most lucrative articles of French export, so much sought after by well-to-do Englishmen in those times, were losing their place on the list of the foreign trade of France.

In the end the population laid the responsibility for their misery at the door of Colbert or his system. The masses, dazed by the war glories of the triumphant French armies in Holland, bestowed the title "Le Grand" on Louis XIV and branded Colbert as an enemy of the people. Possibly his work appeared to be a Huguenot contrivance to ruin agriculture, the nobility, and the Church. For was not manufacture

[1] Quesnay, *Œuvres*, edited by Oncken, p. 357 (note).

introduced and developed by Henry IV ànd his Huguenot ministers?

Colbert's fate brings to memory that of Cardinal Wolsey. Both were highly gifted statesmen of middle-class origin, serving with exemplary devotion ruthless despots. Both brought much greatness to their respective countries. Both were anything but popular with the nation, for they had to bear the odium and the consequences of the extravagance of their respective masters. And both received the *coup de grâce* from monarchs who knew no gratitude. The reproach of thriftlessness or worse, levelled at Colbert by Louis XIV, laid low the statesman, whose uprightness and frugality was never impugned, and whose health was already undermined by more than twenty years of ceaseless labour for the prosperity of France.

In contrast, however, with Wolsey, who was more medieval than many of the national elements of his country and his time, Colbert's economic activity was much in advance of the traditional conceptions which were still prevalent among the nobility, the legal profession, and, of course, the clergy. His manufacturing pace was undoubtedly much too rapid for the great majority of his countrymen, who have always been much more conservative in economics than in politics. He was a progressive townsman of the type of the English mercantilists, whose minds were alienated from the past, whereas he lived and worked among "bourgeois-gentilshommes" and Catholics. It is characteristic that the two medieval-minded French economic writers between the years 1690 and 1770—namely Boisguillebert and Quesnay—though bearing witness to the integrity and good intentions of Colbert,[1] are very critical of his work, while Voltaire is full of praise of his achievements.

Pierre Le Pesant de Boisguillebert, the severest economic critic of the conditions in the reign of Louis XIV, who began to write about a decade after the death of Colbert, while generally condemning the mercantilist doctrines, ascribed the cause of misery for the greater part to the arbitrary and extortionate *taille* and excise, and to a certain degree to the *douanes* (customs duties) or the protectionist policy of the "ministre qui était très intègre." It was the Court and the high personages of the kingdom "qui ont erigé des désordres, ou plûtot la ruine de France."[2] François Quesnay is more severe on Colbert, who, though "tout occupé des manufactures a cru cependant qu'il fallait diminuer la taille," and even desired to assist the farmers, though this could not be reconciled with the needs of the State. Later on Quesnay directly attacks the economics of Colbert and declares: "On n'oubliera jamais qu'un ministre du dernier siècle, ébloui du commerce des Hollandais et de l'éclat des manufactures de luxe, a jété la patrie dans un tel délire que l'on ne parlait plus que commerce et argent. . . . Le ministre, si éstimable par ses bonnes intentions,

---

[1] It may be remarked that neither of the two economists mentions Colbert by name, but refer to him simply as *le ministre*.

[2] Boisguillebert, in Daire's *Economistes-Financiers*, p. 316.

mais trop attaché a ses idées, voulut faire nâitre les richesses du travail des doigts," and thus deranged the whole economic constitution of the kingdom. He obstructed the export of grain in order to make the manufacturer flourish, but ruined agriculture. Quesnay speaks here like a headstrong conservative and pious country squire, to whom the drive and push of the "moneyed interests" are utterly repugnant.[1] Quite different is the opinion of Voltaire: "Colbert," he writes, "deserves to be cherished," for he served his country well, yet the people after his death "voulut déchirer le corps." France, he says, was flourishing till the war of 1689. The French owed to him their industry and their commerce and, consequently, their opulence; and as soon as peace was restored, they would revive again.[2] Neither Boisguillebert's, nor Quesnay's, nor Voltaire's views of Colbert's work need be regarded as impartial, but it is worthy of notice that Voltaire's view coincides with Cantillon's, who was an independent economist and student of French life. He writes: "France grew in power from 1646 (when manufactures of cloth were set up there) to 1684, when the Huguenots (Protestant entrepreneurs and artisans) were driven out of it; since that time France has been receding."[3]

[1] Quesnay, Œuvres, pp. 208, 261–262, 343.
[2] Voltaire, Siècle de Louis XIV, chap. xxviii.
[3] Richard Cantillon, Essai sur la nature du Commerce, ed. Higgs, 1931, pp. 246–247.

5. *Rise of the "Return-to-Nature" Movement*

With the death of Colbert, much of the creative spirit went out of the policy of encouraging manufactures. The bureaucracy had henceforth a free hand to issue edicts, ordinances, and regulations, and appoint inspectors to supervise methods of production. At the death of Colbert the number of those edicts was forty-eight; in 1739 it rose to 230, and it still kept on increasing.

Equally disastrous was the revocation of the edict of Nantes (1685). Though the latter is generally regarded as the effect of Catholic opposition to Protestantism, yet there was in it also the popular reaction against the industrial revolution set on foot by the Huguenots and promoted by Colbert's legislation and general economic activity. In the hostility to Colbert there was undoubtedly a great deal of emotional rebellion of the old agrarian system against the growth of industry and commerce. In the case of the Huguenots the hostility drew additional strength from religious motives. At any rate, the act of revocation expatriated several hundred thousand Protestants, among them the most skilful artisans, manufacturers, enterprising tradesmen and merchants—the agents of the new economy. The decline set in, and was later aggravated by the wars of the Spanish Succession, which imposed unbearable burdens on the agricultural population. After the peace of Utrecht and of the death of Louis XIV (1715), France found herself agriculturally and financially on the brink of ruin, with results which, of course, reacted unfavourably on manufacture.

The whole glorious and glittering period of the Grand Monarch, with its splendours and pageantries, its vistas of palaces and gardens, but also with its devastation of Nature's beauties and bounties in field and vineyard, appeared as poisonous excrescences of an artificial and corrupt civilization.

The depression caused by the disastrous policy of Louis XIV was intensified and deepened by the consequences of the sudden collapse of John Law's monetary system and financial experiments in Paris in the years 1719–1720. Buoyed up with hopes of untold riches to be obtained by means of an inconvertible paper currency, banking establishments, and the foundation of oversea companies, the nation found itself, without any warning and within a short space of time, in the midst of a stupefying crash of the whole fantastic structure.

The French economic historian. J. A. Blanqui, describes the effect of that catastrophe on the nation: "Le triste dénoûment du système de Law laissait la France entière dans une véritable stupeur. On ne savait plus désormais à quels principes se fier, après avoir vu rapidement naître et mourir tant de fortunes. . . . De toutes les valeurs industrielles ecloses sous l'atmosphère embrassée du *système* il ne restait plus que la ruine, la désolation, et la banqueroute."[1] The

[1] J. A. Blanqui, *Histoire de l'Économie Politique*, ed. 1860, chap. 32.

only element of wealth that remained intact was the soil.

The catastrophe of the wars of Louis XIV, the decay of manufactures, and the bursting of Law's opalescent financial bubbles in the first years of the regency could not but leave a series of indelible impressions on the minds of the moral philosophers, poets, and economists.

A profound longing for a simple life, for a more stable foundation of existence, for innocent joys and rustic virtues, for natural justice and freedom—in short, for "a return to nature"—began mightily to stir the imagination and intellects of the nation. Men asked for an "ordre naturel," which meant, in effect, a return to the past or an escape to Utopia.

These impressions and longings were not obliterated by the industrial and commercial revival, which set in a decade or two later. The manufacturers of metals, textiles, porcelain, and silks grew prosperous, the urban population increased, towns were rebuilding, and new life was pulsating.[1] This revival was, however, scattered among various settlements and towns, such as Creusot, Saint-Étienne, Firminy, Lyon, Abbéville, Roubaix, Lille, Limoges, etc., while the indelible impressions of the recent past grew concentrated and found expression in the works of Jean Jacques Rousseau and François Quesnay, the poet and the economist of the "Return to Nature."

The work of Rousseau is outside the scope of these

[1] Germain Martin, *Les grandes industries en France* (1715–1774), Paris, 1900.

pages. Our main task is to deal with the economic teaching of physiocracy, and since those teachings are rooted in the moral philosophy of the law of nature, it is necessary to deal first with this doctrine, which so deeply influenced the whole eighteenth century.

III

THE ECONOMICS OF THE LAW
OF NATURE

1. *Graeco-Roman and Church Teaching*

It is one of the glories of Greek thought that it
gave to humanity the doctrine of the law of nature
(*nomos physei*), the unwritten rights of man, which the
Roman moralists and jurists embodied in *ius naturale*.
This doctrine took man out of his ethnic and political
group, his *gens* or *polis*, and it looked upon him simply
as a living being, a member of universal human society,
who, urged by his impulse of self-preservation, was
procuring for himself those things which he found on
land, on trees, in woods, or in water, and which were
necessary and proper for his bodily existence. The
Greeks and Romans assumed it to be in conformity
with justice that he should freely appropriate for his
use those things, merely by virtue of his having come
into the world. It was his natural right, his birthright,
for in nature there were no severalties. "Sunt autem
privata nulla natura."[1]

The same reasonings were applied to all those im-
pulses, instincts, and needs, which were inherent in
man's bodily nature, and which served his self-
preservation and the continuance of the human species.

[1] Cicero, *de Officiis*, I, VII, 21.

The Greeks and Romans saw mankind in its state of nature, all free and equal, all moved by the same propensities. Man was man before he was bound and limited, or divided into orders and classes, by positive or civil laws and regulations. "By the law of nature mankind are one community and make up one society."[1]

We have until now treated the doctrine of the law of nature as based mainly on the physical characteristics of man. With the spread of Stoic teaching from the third century B.C. and onwards, the doctrine assumed a more spiritual and ethical character. It grew into a part of moral philosophy. Nature was not an expanse of various forms of matter only, but an animated universe, pervaded and filled with divine spirit. God was immanent in nature, whose law was goodness and equity, "bonum et aequum." Man partook of the divine spirit; he was not only a physical but an ethical being, and it was his duty to follow the law of nature.[2]

Man at first followed that law, but his impulse of self-preservation, a purely physical or animal instinct, led in the course of time to greed and lust, to a complicated social state, to a deterioration and corruption of man's behaviour, which rendered necessary the enactment of positive laws in order to make life in society bearable. Positive laws were, however, a poor makeshift, and there would be no happiness until man

[1] John Locke, *Of Civil Government*, § 128.
[2] A. C. Pearson, *Fragments of Zeno*, 1891 (Introduction).

lived in harmony with nature by following its law of goodness and equity.

To the Fathers of the Church, learned in Scripture and in Greek and Roman thought, the doctrine of *ius naturale* must have been congenial. The Biblical lesson concerning the life of Adam in God's garden, his fall from grace, the story of Cain and Abel, could not but appear to them as symbolizing the primeval simplicity and quiet happiness of man, which was destroyed through lust, greed, and envy, through introducing a complicated urban civilization. Disobedience to the law drove man out of the natural state; hard labour was henceforth his lot: Cain, the city builder, killed the shepherd, the personification of the idyllic life of sylvan innocence.

The Church assimilated the doctrine of the law of nature, which forms an important and precious element of Christian theology. The Fathers found support for the adoption of that doctrine in St. Paul, who declares that the Gentiles, though not knowing the law (of Moses), "do by nature the things contained in the Law . . . which show the work of the law written in their hearts, their conscience also bearing witness" (Romans ii. 14–15). And there was in the Graeco-Roman *ius naturale* another feature which was acceptable to the Church—namely, its universalism. There was neither Jew nor Greek, neither Roman nor Goth, but all were human souls in need of salvation. The Fathers and the Schoolmen likewise regarded civil or positive law as an inferior substitute for God's law in the fallen state of man. Finally, they also desired to see the rule of goodness and equity in the commercial dealings between man and man.

2. *Aristotle and Aquinas on Exchanges*

The Fathers and, in a larger measure, the School-men refer to Aristotle as the philosophical authority in all matters of economics,[1] which are treated in his *Ethics* (book v) and in *Politics* (book i, chap. 3, §§ 1–23). According to Aristotle, man is by nature a social animal; at first as a member of his kindred, then of the *polis*. His necessaries he obtains either by his own work in the kindred, and later on, in the *polis*, or by exchanging the goods he has in superfluity for the goods he lacks, or by the medium of money, which was invented to facilitate exchanges. There are, says the philosopher, two kinds of exchanges. One is that of the households and States, which procure goods for the satisfaction of the needs of the families and citizens. They obtain them either by barter or through the medium of money. Such exchanges are natural, that is, rightful; they are performed on the basis of commutative justice, value for value, equality of exchange, without loss to one nor gain to the other, but to the benefit of both, since those transactions enable them to satisfy their needs.[2]

[1] See the author's *Early British Economics*, pp. 18–50, where the teaching of Aristotle and the English Schoolmen is treated more fully.
[2] Cf. Quesnay, *Œuvres*, pp. 151–152, 484, 538): "L'essence du gain véritable entre les hommes ne consiste pas à avoir quelque

There is, however, another sort of exchange. Its purpose is not the satisfaction of natural needs or general demands, but to procure monetary gain. The buyers and sellers are business men. They do not produce the goods, but buy them for money with the intention of selling them for more money. Such exchanges are chrematistic, that is, aiming at getting gold and silver coins, monetary wealth without limit. They are unnatural, for there is no equity in them; their gains bring losses to others; they are based on inequality.

The Fathers and Schoolmen adopted the Aristotelian views, for they coincided with Scriptural ethics. The two passages most quoted in support of those views are the following. It is said in the Psalter (70–71, 15–16): "My mouth shall relate thy righteousness all the day, and also thy salvation, for I have never known trafficking (numbers, accounts) and I shall enter into the glory of God." The second passage is in the Gospel (Matt. xxi. 12): "Jesus went into the temple of God, and cast out all the buyers and sellers, and overthrew the tables of the money changers," by which our Lord

chose pour rien, ce qui est contre les lois de la nature, mais qui consiste toujours dans les échanges de valeur pour valeur égale." . . . "Le commerce n'est qu'un échange de valeur pour valeur égale et que rélativement à ces valeurs il n'y a ni perte ni gain entre les contractants. . . . Le commerce est profitable à tous deux, car tous les deux se procurent la jouissance des richesses."—Another physiocratic writer, Le Trosne, declares: "L'échange est de sa nature un contrat d'égalité qui se fait de valeur pour valeur égale. Il n'est donc pas un moyen de s'énrichir, puisque l'on donne autant que l'on reçoit" (*De l'interêt social* in Daire's *Les Physiocrates*, pp. 903 *et seq.*).

showed that traders and money-mongers could not please God.

St. Thomas Aquinas, the most authoritative School-man dealing with Aristotelian economics, gives the following commentary: "The philosopher says, two-fold is the exchange (*commutatio*) of things; one is quasi natural and necessary, that is, the commutation of a thing for another, or of things for money, for the pur-pose of satisfying the needs of life; such exchanges are not properly the business of *negotiatores*, but of the heads of households and States who have to procure for their families and States all that is necessary for life ("talis commutatio non proprie pertinet ad nego-tiatores, sed magis ad œconomicos vel politicos qui habent providere vel domui vel civitate de rebus necessariis ad vitam"). The other sort of exchanges, which are performed either with money for money (money changers) or with commodities for money aiming at lucre, are *negotiationes* and form the business of *negotiatores*." Or as Aquinas says in another place, "Only he is a trafficker who 'ad hoc emit ut carius vendat.' "[1]

We have thus two kinds of exchanges: "commutatio rei ad rem," and "negotiatio." The former is barter or purchase for satisfying our needs, and therefore an exchange according to the law of nature, that is, right-ful. The other is exchange for the purpose of gain, or doing business in order to sell at a higher price than

[1] Aristotle, *Politics* (I, 3, § 6–21); St. Thomas Aquinas, *Summa, Secunda Secundae*, questio 77, Art. 4, ad 2.

the original purchase price, and therefore an exchange against the law of nature, that is, not in accordance with "bonum et aequum."

The question is now as to their appropriate rendering into English, for obviously they cannot both have the connotation of trading or exchanging, since each Latin term has its individual meaning. "Commutatio," I take it, points etymologically to commerce (*commutatio mercium*), that is, exchange of commodities, either as barter or by the medium of money. The latter is in the meaning of Aristotle and St. Thomas Aquinas a commerce in the local market or home trade for the use of the consumers. Commerce, then, is natural; no taint is attached to it. Different is *negotiatio*, which implies perpetual dealings in merchandise—an interminable series of buying and selling in foreign and home markets for no other purpose than finding the most profitable markets and gaining a favourable monetary balance. The term "negotiatio" would thus most aptly be rendered as "traffic" (lucrative business, *nec-otium*, a restless busy-ness and drive for money). The term "traffic" is often met with in mercantilist writings. *Treasure of Traffike* by Lewes Roberts, London (1641), is one of the source books of mercantilism. *Negotiatio*, or traffic, would thus imply mainly foreign trade, carried on for the purpose of gain or increasing one's riches; while commerce was mainly home trade, carried on for ministering to the bodily needs of one's neighbours.

We shall find later on that François Quesnay and

his commentator, Le Mercier de la Rivière,[1] in their disquisitions on commerce, adhere to those definitions of commerce and traffic, though Quesnay in the first years of his economic studies was not as consistent in the distinctive use of the terms as in his later economic writings. Both writers emphasize the moral difference between those two branches of trading. The Scholastic influence, particularly that of Aquinas, on the leading physiocrats is striking, and its recognition will assist us to solve the riddle of physiocracy. It pervades all economic and political reasonings of Quesnay. His works read in the light of *ius naturale* and Aristotelian and Schoolmen's ethics, as a reaction against mercantilism, gain much in rationality and consistency— qualities which they lack if read as eighteenth-century economics.

3. *Aquinas on Traffic (Foreign Trade)*

St. Augustin, in his sermon (*Enarratio*) on Psalm 70, made an attempt to justify the moderate gain of the trafficker by pointing out that his service in equalizing supplies and his risk and trouble in rendering that

[1] Le Mercier, the most authoritative commentator of Quesnay, writes: "*Trafiquer* n'est pas *commercer*. On *trafique* quand on achète et revend les marchandises dont d'autres hommes sont premiers propriétaires; on *commerce* quand on tire de son propre fonds, les marchandises qu'on échange contre les valeurs quelconques, en autres marchandises ou en argent. Ainsi celui qui *trafique* n'est qu'une espèce de salarié, qui, par son industrie, parvient à s'approprier une portion des richesses des autre hommes; et ceux qui *commercent*, ne font en cela, que jouir de leurs propres richesses" (*L'Ordre naturel et essentiel*), ed. 1910, p. 260.

service to the community, deserves to be rewarded, for the labourer is worthy of his hire. This argument was taken up by many Schoolmen, and they made such a gain lawful.[1] Aquinas deals with the subject in his *Summa* (*Secunda Secundae*, questio 77). As it is usual with Schoolmen, Aquinas first refers to those early Christian writers, such as Chrysostom (or pseudo-Chrysostom) and Cassiodor, who altogether condemn gainful trading. Then he confronts those views with those of St. Augustin, and finally Aquinas himself gives his "Response" and says substantially:

The Philosopher differentiates between the two exchanges: one is natural, for it serves the needs of our fellow-citizens, that is, it supplies goods for the purpose of consumption, but the other sort of exchange (aiming at money-making) is denounced, because it is *per se* intended to serve the greed of gain, without limits. Therefore, says Aquinas, "negotiatio" considered in itself contains a certain turpitude, inasmuch as it does not *per se* imply any honest and necessary aim and end: "Lucrum enim quod est negotiationis finis"; while it does not in itself involve anything honourable or necessary it has also *per se* nothing that is vicious or contrary to virtue. Traffic, in serving the country by bringing goods where they are abundant to a country where they are deficient, deserves a moderate gain. Still, it may be remarked that clergymen ought to abstain not only from things that are in themselves evil, but also from things "quae habent

[1] See the author's *Early British Economics*, pp. 28 *et seq.*

speciem mali" (which have the appearance of evil). And this applies to traffic ("in negotiatione contingit") because of the vices which are often found in persons engaged in trade, as it is said in Eccles. xxvi. 28), "A huckster is hardly free from sins of lips." Trade entangles the soul too much in earthly matters and withdraws it from spiritual contemplation.

More decisive in his censure on traffickers or foreign trade is Aquinas in his *De regimine principum* (book ii, chap. 3), where the attitude of government towards the economic life of the State is dealt with. States are supplied either from their own resources or by way of foreign trade. It is manifest that the former way is preferable, both from reasons of safety and morality. In case of war, self-sufficiency secures the inhabitants from many hardships which may arise from difficulties of transport or stoppage of imports. In peace times it is likewise better for the country to have an abundance of its own, for if it is deficient in many commodities it must necessarily have recourse to foreign trade, which leads to a corruption of the morals of the many citizens. The alien *negotiatores* bring in their laws, customs, and ways of life to the injury of the State, and if the citizens follow the example of the foreign traders the harmonious inter-course among the citizens is disturbed. Moreover, if the citizens themselves take to trading, the door is opened to many vices. For the greatest zeal of the *negotiatores* is directed towards acquiring lucre, whereby cupidity finds entrance into the hearts of the citizens, the consequence of which is that everything becomes venal. Faithfulness decreases and frauds multiply; the public good is disregarded, for everybody seeks only his own particular advantage; the love of civic virtue disappears when honour, the reward of virtue, is conferred upon all those persons. In such a State civic intercourse becomes necessarily corrupt.

Trade, besides, weakens the stamina of man and makes him unfit for military service. The *negotiatores*, in pursuing a shadow (money) abandon labour, and while indulging in luxuries they enervate spirit and body. It is therefore better and worthier that the necessaries of the State should be supplied from its own territory, than that it should depend on foreign trade. There is, however, no State which could produce from its own lands all its needs. Some foreign trade will be necessary for a State, either for the purpose of carrying away the surplus of its produce or to bring in some goods which it lacks. But the number of *negotiatores* should be moderate.

Foreign trade, then, is a sort of evil, though a necessary evil—a makeshift to be used sparingly.[1]

---

[1] Quesnay is fully in accord with those views of Aquinas. He declares: "Le commerce extérieur est un pis-aller pour les nations auxquelles le commerce intérieur ne suffit pas pour débiter avantageusement les productions de leur pays. . . . Les interêts des negociants-revendeurs et ceux de la nation sont très opposés. . . . Le commerçant tend à acheter au plus bas prix possible, afin d'étendre son bénéfice le plus possible aux dépens de la nation" (*Œuvres*, pp. 484, 467, 323). Le Mercier writes: "Je conviens donc que le commerce extérieur peut être indispensable, par rapport à quelques productions étrangères . . . ; sous ce point de vue nous devons dire que le commerce extérieur est *un mal necéssaire*

4. *Natural Occupation, Value and Price*

Of the activities of man to acquire the things which he needs to sustain the life of his household or to maintain the life of the citizens of a State, there is one, says Aristotle, which is natural. We must suppose that those things either existed prior to the activities of man or that they are made by man from the materials provided by nature. Those things are true wealth, since the desire for them ceases as soon as man's appetites are satisfied, that is, the amount of property needed for a good life is limited by man's natural needs for food, shelter, and raiment. These are real goods, since the demand for them is general; they supply human wants; they are indispensable to bodily existence; the source of those things are the soil and its fruits.[1] Agriculture and cattle raising are the most natural modes of life. The greatest number of people obtain a living from the fruits of the soil. Such are the modes

(*L'Ordre naturel*, ed. 1910, p. 266). Abbé Bandeau defines commerce and traffic (Daire, *Les Physiocrates*, pp. 726–727): "Nous confondons le *traffic*, qui n'est qu'un accessoire, avec le *commerce* souvent très utile, quelquefois même presque indispensable. Acheter des productions . . . de mains de ceux qui les ont produites pour les revendre . . . c'est ce qui characterise le traffic ou le negoce." The Hollanders, it is said, are doing a flourishing "commerce," in reality they are traffickers, that is, middlemen between producers and consumers in different parts of Europe.

On the economics of St. Thomas Aquinas see Schreiber, *Volks-Wirtschaftliche Anschauungen der Scholastik*, Jena, 1913; Joseph Rickaby, *Aquinas Ethicus*, 1892; *id. Moral Philosophy*, ed. 1901, or any other edition.

[1] Cf. Quesnay (*Œuvres*, p. 468): "Les vraies richesses sont les produits qui renaissent annuellement de la terre."

of subsistence which prevail among those whose industry is employed immediately upon the products of nature, and whose food is not acquired by exchange (Aristotle, *Politics* I, 2, §§ 1, 2; I, 8, §§ 7, 13; *Ethics* I, chap. 1).

Aristotle's opinion was preceded and even more clearly expressed by that of Socrates, who, according to Xenophon (*Œconomicos*, chap. v), declared: "What art rewards the labourer more generously than tillage? . . . Husbandry is the mother and nurse of all other arts. For, when husbandry flourishes, all other arts flourish, but whenever the land is laid waste, the other arts . . . well-nigh perish." Xenophon quotes Socrates' view on property (wealth) and its increase, which is relevant to our subject. "Property is that which is useful for supplying a livelihood. . . . The knowledge of husbandry appears to be that by which men can increase estates" (*ibid.*, chap. vi). Socrates and Aristotle are followed by Cicero, who regards agriculture not only the most natural occupation but also the most proper to acquire wealth. None is better for that purpose than tillage, and none is more profitable, salutary, and pleasurable (*de Officiis*, book i, 151).

Aquinas, as we have just noticed, supports the view that it is much more becoming (*dignior*) for a *civitas* to supply its needs from its own fields than to be dependent on traffic (*De regimine principum*, book ii, chap. 3).

Agriculture, then, is the source of real riches. It is the most productive of wealth. It ought to form the foundation of every commonwealth. Riches consist in those things which satisfy human needs—in other words, riches consist in goods, that is, in things which everybody wants, for which there is a general demand:[1] "Bonum est quod omnia appetunt."

It is this general demand which makes them valuable, or gives them value. Since, however, no individual can produce all the goods he wants, and even no commonwealth can obtain from its own lands all it needs, exchange must take place, either in a direct manner through barter or through the medium of money.

The law of nature requires that the exchanges should be equal: value for value, utility for utility. But how should we measure the values of the goods, so as to make the exchanges equal? In order to equalize exchanges it was agreed among men to make money the measure of value. It should show that the goods, which are being exchanged one for another, possess equal value.

Money, thus being only a medium and a measure which men instituted by consent and convention, is not natural wealth, is not a "good" by nature, but by man-made law. Money is artificial wealth, for in the absence of real wealth no amount of money could ward off starvation, or give shelter from the inclemency of the weather.

[1] Cf. Quesnay's *Œuvres*, pp. 245–246: "Les terres ne sont des richesses que parce que leurs productions sont nécessaires pour satisfaire aux besoins des hommes et que ce sont ces besoins eux-mêmes qui établissent les richesses."

It was said above that justice must be a basis of exchange: equality of value, that is, equality of demand or utility. Failing equality, the buyer or seller, the producer or consumer must suffer loss. If a farmer or craftsman does not receive in return his expenses and the value of his labour, there can be no doubt that in the long run tillage will deteriorate and arts and crafts will perish. This is also the opinion of Aristotle and his commentator, Aquinas. "Doomed to destruction," writes the latter, "are arts and crafts, if the artisan who makes a commodity (*artificium*) fails to receive for it so much in quantity and quality as he had put into it" (Aquinas, Commentary on Aristotle's *Ethics*, book v, lectio 7). Aquinas demands the "just price," that is, the money which the farmer or artisan receives for his commodity, should be equal to the expenses or the labour spent on the commodity; he should be able to obtain for the money a commodity of equal value. As it was difficult for individual tradespeople and craftsmen to find the just price, medieval authorities had the duty to determine it. "Those who govern the State," declares Aquinas, "should determine the just price of marketable commodities with due consideration of time and place" (*Summa, Secunda Secundae,* questio 77, art. 1, 2).

The statutory prices fixed by public authorities were based on commutative justice, or retribution of expenses and labour. This can be seen from the English assize of bread and ale, which functioned for many centuries. The justices ascertained first the market price of wheat and malt, which the baker and brewer paid for those raw materials; then they added the expenses incurred in carriage and in baking or brewing; finally, they added the value of the labour which the baker and brewer spent in the production of bread and ale. There was no "gain" or "profit," but a wage or a salary for the services rendered by baker and brewer to the community.

In the economics of the law of nature, ancient and medieval (Schoolmen and Canon lawyers), value consisted in utility, that is, in the capacity of a thing to satisfy a general demand, a general need.[1] Price consisted in the cost of labour and amount of expenses required for the production of a commodity.[2] There was no "gain," no "profit," but the prime cost of production. The making or manufacturing of commodities did not add new wealth, but transformed the existing elements of wealth, or gave them new forms. In short, they were unproductive or sterile.

5. *The Schoolmen and Locke on Property*

There is, as a rule, some core of truth in historic traditions, though it comes to us adorned by poetic or romantic imagination, and shaped by the transmitters according to their wishes and ideas. And there is surely a core of truth in the state of nature tradition, which Hebrew, Hellenic, and Roman writers handed

[1] See the author's *Early British Economics*, p. 166.
[2] *Ibid.*, p. 230.

down to European humanity. The law of nature doctrine is nothing else than a theoretical abstraction of the immemorial customs and ways of life of tribal society, which preceded civil society. The doctrine was accepted and reasoned upon by medieval theologians and woven into romance by medieval poets. Later on the moral philosophers made it the foundation of their constitutional theories, particularly after the discovery of the various tribal societies in America, which appeared to offer an irrefutable demonstration of the truth of the doctrine.

The doctrine contained, however, a view of property which was difficult to reconcile with prevailing conditions. The law of nature declared that there is no private property in nature. How, then, did the division of things arise, and seeing that it exists, does it exist lawfully?

The Schoolmen, without any exception, answered the question by pointing out that as long as the state of nature lasted all things were common, for nobody took more than he needed for satisfying his bodily needs. After the Fall of man, when greed and selfishness increased, the law concerning community of things was revoked, lest the greedy and violent should seize everything and make social life impossible. In order to protect themselves and secure their natural rights, men agreed to set up an authority, a civil government, and to invest it with legislative and executive power necessary to make peace and unity prevail. This authority divided the earth or its fullness into severalties. It was thus by man-made law that the property arose. Since, however, government was instituted by the consent or election of the men themselves, it is a quasi-natural arrangement and therefore lawful and its acts are lawful.

Government (or State), the division of things (or property), inequality and restraint, thus arose in consequence of the corruption of man, and though those institutions which form civil society or civilization were made lawful through consent and agreement of men, they are none the less tainted with sin. We find the same views on civilization in the writings of Bois-guillebert, the precursor of physiocracy, particularly in his *Dissertation sur les richesses* (1707).

Those views on property were, however, modified by the influence of John Locke, whose endeavour it was to justify civil society and to remove from its origin all taint of sin. Locke's argument is developed in his *Essay on Civil Government*.

Men, by reason of having been born, have a natural right to self-preservation and consequently to sustenance, which they can obtain from the earth and its fruits, for in the state of nature there are no exclusive rights. God has given the earth to mankind, to the sons of man, as it is said in Psalm cxv. 16. The earth thus being given for the use of men, there must be a means for the individual man to appropriate the fruits in order to enjoy them or a piece of land to grow them. This appropriation took place in the state of nature, that is, prior to men instituting government. And the appropriation was quite rightful, since man, being born free, has unquestionably a property in his own person. The labour of his body, the work of his hands, are the efforts of his person. Man, in removing things from the common store of nature by his labour, joins to them his own personality and gives them most of the value which they possess after man's labour had prepared them for use. The land, when cultivated and improved by labour, exceeds by far the value of it when it lay in common. In most things ninety-nine hundredths of value are due to labour and one hundredth to nature. And since labour is unquestionably the property of the labourer, the product of his labour is rightfully his property. Labour made distinct titles to several parcels of land for private use. "From all this it is evident that, though the things of nature are given in common, yet man, by being master of himself and proprietor of his own person and labour, has in himself the great foundation of property. This labour, in the beginning, gave a right of property, whenever anyone was pleased to employ it upon what was common" ($\S\S$ 38–45).

Thus the right of property arose "in the beginning," that is, in the state of nature.[1] But how did inequality arise? Man, as we know, was born not only free but equal, with equal rights to property.

[1] This argument was fully accepted by the physiocrats. Le Mercier, the foremost commentator of their doctrines, writes: "C'est donc de la nature même que chaque homme tient la propriété exclusive de sa personne, et celle des choses acquises par ses recherches et ses travaux" (*L'Ordre Naturel*, ed. 1910, p. 9).

Men, though born with equal rights, are not equally endowed by nature. Some are more industrious than others, or more provident than others. Some could thus gather more fruits from the trees or bushes or produce more corn from the soil and thus obtain more goods, but those goods being perishable, nobody took the trouble to gather or produce or accumulate more than he needed. And if some had a superfluity of goods, they bartered them for the things which they were lacking, or for things which were less perishable and could be kept for times of need or for future exchanges. As long as such a durable and easily exchangeable thing was not available, the industrious and provident cared little for accumulating perishable things. The inequalities, if such arose, were inconsiderable and of no account.

Finally, however, men found that gold and silver would answer the purpose, for they were durable and easily exchangeable, and by consent and agreement men set a value upon them, or in other words, money was invented. With this invention, the industrious and provident could start accumulating goods from the soil and from the trees, for they could exchange their superfluities for durable goods—for gold and silver money. Now, says Locke, "find out something that hath the use and value of money amongst the neighbours, you shall see the same man will begin presently to enlarge his possessions" (§ 49), and inequality of property will inevitably be the result. Since, however, continues Locke in his curious logic, money was invented and introduced by agreement and consent, from which inequalities resulted, men have also by implication consented and agreed to inequality. All this happened when man was still in the state of nature, outside the bounds of civil or political society. Property and inequality, then, arose in the state of nature and are therefore unquestionably rightful.

It was only after those natural arrangements had been instituted that men, in order to ward off invasions of their rights by the corrupted and vicious, agreed or consented to form a government or a civil society "for the mutual preservation of their lives, liberties, and estates," which, says Locke, "I call by the general name, property. The great and chief end therefore of men's uniting into Commonwealths, and putting themselves under government is the preservation of property" (§§ 123–124), and to secure peace, safety, and public good of the people.

To sum up this chapter in a single sentence: The physiocrats accepted the universalist outlook from the Stoics and Christianity; the views on agriculture exchange, price, and traffic from Aristotle and Aquinas; and the reasonings of Locke on property and the rise of civil society to protect life, liberty, and property.

IV

PIONEERS OF PHYSIOCRACY

1. *English Contribution to the Doctrine*

The opposition to the restrictions on the corn trade as well as to the mercantilist policy of favouring manufacture at the expense of agriculture took its rise in the ranks of the English landed interest. It was among them that the thesis originated that the land, and not manufacture, was the real and only source of the wealth of the realm. And it was also among them that the demand for complete freedom of trade was first formulated.

In England those ideas remained isolated. The reasonings, which later on established the main tenets of French physiocracy, arose from particular grievances, and they aimed only at removing certain statutes, at easing the restraints that impeded the growth of trade and commerce. They were not condensed into a doctrine, and they left little trace on eighteenth-century English economists. What there is of physiocratic ideas in Adam Smith's main work came admittedly from French sources.

In France the fundamental tenets of physiocracy, which arose there quite independently, were elaborated into a system of social criticism and social reconstruction. They were grounded in universalist ethics, in the moral philosophy of *ius naturale*, and in the teaching of the Schoolmen, particularly of St. Thomas Aquinas. They formed a school and later a sect, something like the German and English Marxists at the turn of the twentieth century.

The economic germ of physiocracy is contained in the following lines, written by an anonymous English author in 1676:

"It is manifest that it is the greatest concern and interest of the nation to preserve the nobility and gentry and those to whom the land of this country belongs, at least much greater than (to preserve) the few artificers employed in the working of superfluity of our wool, or the merchants who gain by the exportation of our manufacture: (i) Because they are masters and proprietors of the foundation of all the wealth of this nation, all the profits arising out of the ground which is theirs. (ii) Because they bear all the taxes and public burdens. . . . (iii) Because they maintain great families which conduce much to the consumption of our manufactures. . . . (iv) Because they must of necessity bear all magistracies and public employments, and are the only hindrances of the confusion which would follow from equality."[1]

The point most relevant to our subject is to be found in the anonymous author's statement that the earth is the source of all wealth and that all the profits

[1] *Reasons for a Limited Exportation of Wool*, London, 1676, p. 5. British Museum Reading Room Catalogue, *Tracts on Wool*, press mark 712, g. 16.

arise from the soil. This is also the economic essence of the physiocratic doctrine of the *produit net*, that is, that agriculture is the only productive occupation, covering not only the prime cost of production but producing a surplus or profits, an increase of riches. We have also in these statements the rationale of the single tax, since, as the author avers, the landowners bear all the taxes and public burdens—a view which was in those times widespread, for we find it in John Locke and Charles Davenant.[1]

The anonymous author demanded that at least a certain proportion of the wool should be given free exportation.

The demand for freer trade in agricultural produce was an old one. Since the end of the fourteenth century the Commons asked for free exportation of corn. In the middle of the sixteenth century several writers, among them John Hales, the first English political economist, pleaded warmly for making corn a merchandise. The husbandman should have the liberty to sell his corn "as freely as men maie doe their other things."[2] In the second half of the seventeenth century the wool growers joined the movement against prohibitions, which grew in strength from the alliance of the landed interests with the overseas mer-

[1] John Locke, *Works*, ed. 1727, vol. iv, p. 27; Charles Davenant, *Works*, 1771, vol. i, pp. 77, 269. Voltaire is of the same opinion. Writing about the physiocrats, he declares: "Il est bien certain que la terre paye tout; quel homme n'est-il-pas convaincu de cette verité? (quoted by Weulersee, *Le Mouvement Physiocratique*, vol. i, 147).

[2] John Hales, *A Discourse of the Commonweal*, ed. 1893, p. 50.

chants (East India Company, Turkey Company, etc.), whose commerce was obstructed by embargoes on coin and bullion exportation. The initial success of the combined movement came in 1663, when, by 15 Caroli II, chap. 7, § 9, the restrictions on the exportation of foreign coin and bullion were eased and at the same date, by 15 Caroli II, chap. 7, § 3, the home corn market was in a certain measure made free and open, that is, the trader could buy up and keep corn stored.[1] Still, even with those facilities, the corn trade languished and the exportation of corn was inconsiderable as it had been in medieval and early modern times, for in all those centuries English agriculture was carried on mainly with a view to home consumption. It was only after the Bounty Act of May 1689 (1 Will. and Mary, chap. 12) had been some years in force that England began to export corn in considerable quantities. Charles Davenant, in his Report to the Commissioners of Trade (December 1711), writes as follows:

"I crave leave to observe that corn is in a manner a new exportation (arising to us from the war), which has in other countries so employed the hands of their people. Formerly we carried grain from the Port of

[1] "The old laws," writes Charles Smith (*Corn Trade*, ed. 1804, p. 74), "which were made before commerce was well understood, those, to wit, 5 & 6 Edw. VI and 5 Eliz., laid many restraints upon the purchasers of corn. In order to abate the rigour of those laws there was passed a law in 15 Caroli II, whereby it was enacted (chap. 7, § 4) 'that when the prices of corn do not exceed the quarters wheat 48/–, rye 32/–, then it shall be lawful for any person to buy in open market and sell it or keep it'; 'the corn trade was made in a manner free and open.'" The said Smith was a London corn-monger and J.P.

London, and but in small quantities." For the year
1662 to 1663 the value of the corn export was estimated at £4,315 5s. 0d.; for 1668 to 1669 at
£2,011 4s. 0d., while in the years 1699 to 1710 (the
years of the war of the Spanish Succession) the export
of grain rose very considerably and amounted in the
annual average ("by a medium of eleven years") to
£274,144 10s. 10d. Those were the years, in which
French agriculture was suffering a calamitous deterioration, which will be dealt with later on, for it
largely contributed to the rise of physiocracy. Meanwhile, we have to notice the legacy which the free
trade demands of the English landed interests left to
English economics, as far as physiocratic ideas are
concerned.

It is noteworthy, and Professor William Ashley has
called attention to it in a paper entitled "Tory Free
Trade," that at the end of the seventeenth century all
ideas concerning free trade and anti-mercantilism came
from Tories,[1] whose prominent writers were Sir
Dudley North and Sir Charles Davenant, and both
preceded the free trade reasonings of the French
physiocrats, who demanded *laissez-faire*, that is, to
leave natural liberty free to function in all matters of
trade and commerce, North's main ideas are expressed
in the following sentences: "In matters of trade the
whole world is but one nation or people, and therein
nations (are) as persons. . . . Laws restraining trade,
foreign or domestic, relating money or other mer-

[1] William Ashley, *Surveys*, 1900, pp. 268 *et seq.*

chandise, are not ingredients to make a people rich. . . . No people ever yet grew rich by policies, but it is peace, industry,[1] and freedom that bring trade and wealth."[2] And the central idea of Davenant is that "trade is in its nature free, finds its own channels, and best directs its own course; and all laws to give it rules and direction may serve private ends, but are seldom advantageous to the public."[3]

2. *Fénelon as Social Critic*

Sober and constructive was, as we have just noticed, the expression of the critical attitude of English writers towards some aspects and effects of mercantilist policy. England, at the end of the seventeenth century, had long since left behind the mirage of utopias, the concomitant of decisive transition periods, which give voice, poetical and romantic, to the dissatisfaction aroused by the economic changes and shifting of social strata. The Glorious Revolution marked the last stage in the process of readjustment.

It was different in France. In religion she overcame all attempts at Protestant reformation, and returned to the medieval Church; in constitutional matters she was at the end of the seventeenth century what England

[1] "Industry" in its literal meaning of "diligent application," and not its secondary meaning of "manufacturing or industrial activity."

[2] Dudley North, *Discourse Upon Trade*, 1691, p. 29.

[3] Charles Davenant, *Works*, 1771, vol. i, pp. 98, 104; vol. v, pp. 424, 452–453.

had been in the sixteenth century. The spiritual and political atmosphere was static, while the growth of manufacture and traffic was moving onwards. Tillage was subordinated to manufacture; the importance of the industrial towns increased at the expense of the countryside; the commercial and foreign policy generated conflicts and wars with the neighbouring nations, which made inordinate demands on the lives and fortunes of the population. The inevitable result was a social ferment, which, in consequence of the suppression of all liberty by Louis XIV, could find no other vent than in utopias, and criticism surcharged with emotion. In the years 1676 to 1710 there were written the utopias, *Histoire des Severambes*, by Vairasse d'Allais, *Terre australe connue*, by Gabriel de Foigny, *Voyages et aventures*, by J. Massé; then the *Testament de Jean Meslier*, a powerful but strongly emotional indictment of the social and political conditions of the period.

Fénelon and Boisguillebert, both of whom wrote in the last decade of the seventeenth century, are more germane to our subject and demand greater attention. Fénelon, armed with the intellectual and humanist culture of the French Church, chose the form of antique dialogue and utopian description. Appointed in 1689 as tutor to the heir presumptive, he attempted to instruct his pupil in the principles of Christian kingship, and royal government according to the law of nature. He did this in form of dialogues between antique philosophers and statesmen (*Dialogues des*

Morts) and of an epic tale about Telemachus, the son of Ulysses, and Mentor. Both works are disguised censures on the warlike policy and commercial nationalism of Louis XIV.

The student of economic history, on leaving mercantilist tracts for physiocratic writings, is struck at once by the universalism of the latter. The narrow boundaries of selfish nationalist existence disappear. In the light of the law of nature, we see man as a member of humanity, either following, with his fellow-men, natural pursuits in peace and happiness, or striving to find a way out of the unnatural environment in which he had become entangled by the lust of money, by the desire for *objets de luxe*, or seeking to return to agriculture and cattle breeding, the never-failing sources of true wealth.

In one of the dialogues between Socrates and Alcibiades the former defends human rights against national rights. "Le droit de conquête est moins fort que celui de l'humanité. . . . Un peuple n'est pas moins un membre de genre humain, qui est la société générale, qu'une famille est un membre d'une nation particulière. Chacun doit incomparablement plus au genre humain, qui est la grande patrie, qu'à la patrie particulière dont il est né. . . . Renoncer au sentiment d'humanité c'est tomber dans la barbarie, . . . ce n'est plus être homme, mais anthropophage."[1]

The same sentiment is expressed in *Telemachus* (book xi): The whole race of man is but one family

[1] Fénelon, *Dialogues des Morts*, ed. 1718, p. 74.

widely scattered upon the earth. All mankind are brothers, and should be mutually endeared by a brother's love; accursed be those impious barbarians who seek for glory in the kindred blood, which is indeed our own. War, indeed, is sometimes a necessity, but the necessity of war is a reproach to man.

Books x–xiii contain in form of a utopia the destructive criticism and the constructive proposals to be applied to our civilization. Idomeneus, a king of a Cretan province, made war upon a neighbouring savage (primitive) tribe who inhabited the fertile coast. The savages left their land and settled in the mountains, but some of the men of Idomeneus followed them even into the mountains, but were made prisoner by the savages. The latter took no revenge, but said to the prisoners: "You have fallen into our hands and we have it in our power to destroy you, but we will not dip our hands in the blood of those who, though strangers, share one common nature with ourselves. Go, then, in peace."

Mentor then takes Idomeneus to task for misgoverning the realm. The population and agriculture, the two pillars of society, had deteriorated. Vast tracts of land lay uncultivated. Artisans were filling the towns, while the number of cultivators was decreasing. Apostrophizing the king, Mentor reproves him, saying: "To gain the appearance of grandeur, you have sapped the foundations of substantial greatness. Correct these errors, and don't delay; suspend all those works of idle magnificence; away with your pomp.

You have been hurried by ambition to the brink of a precipice."

In order to reform the *civitas*, it was first of all necessary to inquire into the state of the country—how many of the inhabitants were occupied in husbandry, how much corn, wine, oil, and other utilities the land could produce for the subsistence of the population, and whether the production would be sufficient or yielding a surplus for the exchange with other goods. We ought likewise to know the countries with which we were carrying on commerce, what merchandise they exported to our country, and what they took from us.

Mentor proposed a number of reforms.

The plough is once more to be held in honour, and the burden of taxation imposed on the cultivators should be eased. Arts and crafts to be limited to work indispensable to life. The number of artisans should accordingly be reduced, and the redundant ones transferred to the countryside, where sufficient land should be given to them for subsistence. The holdings should be of moderate size; there ought not be a landless family in the country. The larger the number of cultivators, the greater the prosperity and happiness of the people.

Commerce should be freed from all duties and impositions which restrict or hinder the circulation of goods among the inhabitants of the earth. But the traffickers should not be free to ply their trade as they think proper. Their number should be reduced, and they should be put under the obligation to produce the accounts of their assets, expenses, and profits. They are to be forbidden to flood the country with apparel of gold and silver, silks of foreign manufacture, *objets de luxe*, vanities, etc., which corrupt and impoverish the inhabitants. A noble simplicity should mark the life and manners of the community.

Those reforms were introduced in the community of Salentum and it prospered greatly. Peace and happiness were the reward of living according to nature.

The political and ethical principles of Fénelon were evidently those propounded by Aquinas in his *De regimine principum*. The community of Salentum was intended to represent their realization. But politics and ethics do not by themselves establish the economic soundness of such a community. An imaginary commonwealth may charm and entertain our emotions, and for a short time even sway our volition, but ultimately it must fail unless it can stand the test of reasonings based on economic realities. To supply this gap was the mission which the physiocrats undertook to fulfil. The first pioneering attempt to support medieval politics and social ethics by economic reasoning was that of Boisguillebert, the contemporary of Fénelon, as well as of Dudley North and Davenant.

3. *Boisguillebert, the Precursor of Quesnay*

(a) *Life and Character.*—Pierre le Pesant, sieur de Boisguillebert, was born in 1646 in Normandy. His family was of the *noblesse de robe*, and related to Corneille. Pierre received his education at a Jesuit college in Rouen, and continued his studies at the famous Port Royal and then at the École de Droit, where he qualified himself for the career of an *avocat*. His first occupation was, however, historical research. He translated the works of Dion Cassius, and wrote a life of Maria Stuart (1674).

Deeply religious, and of an enthusiastic and emotional temperament, he was easily aroused to indignation at acts of injustice, and as easily moved to commiseration with those on whom they were committed. A disposition of that kind might have qualified him solely for the mission of a zealous social reformer rather than for that of an economic investigator, but he possessed also sound business abilities, which stood him in good stead when he was engaged for over ten years (1678–1689) in agriculture and commerce. He acquired in these years a considerable fortune, which helped him to reach the goal to which so many wealthy and educated middle-class Frenchmen in those times aspired—the purchase of an official position. He obtained a high judicial post in the bailiwick of Rouen, where his missionary temperament soon came uppermost, and turned him into a fearless critic of the government. Feverishly active in everything he undertook, he strained at the leash of bureaucratic routine, with the inevitable result that he became unpopular with his colleagues and superiors. They thought him ungovernable and domineering—a rebel against the traditional rules and manners to be observed by high officials.

Boisguillebert and Fénelon were probably the only writers who, as subjects of Louis XIV, had the courage to abstain from joining the chorus of praise bestowed on that monarch. Both drew upon identical sources— Catholic theology, Canon Law, and *ius naturale*; but while Fénelon, as Archbishop of Cambrai, could always rely for protection on the influence of the Church, Boisguillebert stood alone, relying only upon himself, and, therefore, fully exposed to the wrath of his king. It required the courage and devotion of a martyr to stand up for the rights of the labouring people. He was a great Frenchman.

The most productive period of Boisguillebert's literary activity lay between 1695 and 1707. Apart from shorter treatises and papers, he published *Détail de la France* (1697) which contains his main ideas; he re-wrote and enriched it in his *Traité des Grains*, both of which influenced Quesnay. Then came from his pen *Dissertation sur les richesses*, which would be a credit even to Rousseau; finally *Factum de la France* (1707), likewise a restatement of his original *Détail*. In 1707 the forbearance of his superiors reached its limit. His books were proscribed, and their author was exiled to Auvergne for six months and deprived of his office. He died in 1714 in Rouen.

Boisguillebert's books went through several editions during his lifetime. A collective edition of the four books enumerated above was published by E. Daire in *Économistes-Financiers*, Paris, 1843, which is used and referred to in brackets in the following pages.

(*b*) *Social Principles.*—All the writings of Boisguille-bert are pervaded by the conception of the unity of mankind, of an universal humanity, which in its pristine state is governed by inherent laws of nature or Providence. Nature knows no different nationalities, states, or sovereignties, and takes no notice of political boundaries (pp. 386, 388, 410). "La nature aimé également tous les hommes. . . . Elle ne connaît ni différents états, ni différentes souverainetés." Mankind is like a human body, whose various organs serve one another, each doing its work for the well-being of the whole. There is a harmony of interests between all orders and professions, a universal solidarity (*intérêt solidaire*), an equilibrium of the social forces, provided man allows nature to function freely, or as long as man does not deal unjustly with his fellow-man in his natural desire for subsistence.

To secure that harmony and equilibrium, it is not necessary for man to substitute his pseudo-wisdom (*prétendue sagesse*) for the laws of nature; it is only necessary to cease to do violence to nature, "qui tend toujours à la liberté. . . . La nature ne respire que la liberté" (pp. 388–390). Man's daily intercourse with his fellow-man is for the purpose of mutually exchanging their goods and services, so that each can obtain his subsistence. In a natural order the basis of exchange is justice, which is nothing else but reciprocity of requital; each receives back his expenses and cost of labour, without loss or gain, which might injure the other. It is necessary that the balance should be equal in all commercial transactions. Both scales—sale and purchase—should be level (p. 363), so that everybody should equally benefit (p. 355). If, however, the balance is unequal, if one party tries to sell more than he buys, that is, to obtain more than he gives, the basis of exchange, i.e. justice, suffers violence, the equilibrium is destroyed, and disorder follows, with its inescapable concomitants—unhappiness and misery. For, if one loses, if even the humblest worker is wronged, the loss communicates itself, like an infection, to the whole series of exchanges and corrupts all (p. 310). This applies not only to the commercial transactions between individuals, but also to those between province and province, between realm and realm throughout the world (p. 284). Though frontiers divide them they are all interdependent.

To ensure justice in exchanges, no police nor authoritative regulations are necessary. "La nature, ou la Providence, peut seul faire observer la justice, pourvu que qui que ce soit autre ne se'n mêle." The most effective police is liberty of exchanges, that is, free competition. When both parties are free to settle their exchanges of goods or services, when no external compulsion, no privilege or monopoly restrict or "regulate" their transaction and are thus able to negotiate on equal terms, it will ultimately be right reason to which both will appeal as the final arbiter.

Boisguillebert describes that process by showing how Nature works: she established first an equal necessity, an equal interest for all to sell and to buy, to undertake all sorts of commerce, with the intention to profit by the transaction; the desire for profiting moves equally all the markets of the sellers as well as the buyers; the two scales of the balance oscillate according to the forces pressing upon them, and they are balancing the prospects of profit or loss: "et c'est a l'aide de cet équilibre et de cette balance que l'un et l'autre soient également forcés d'entendre raison et s'y soumettre" (p. 409).

The same considerations apply to the manufacturing of commodities. Perfection will not be achieved by edicts, ordinances, and police rules, but by giving the craftsmen free scope for competing with one another. Emulation, the desire to excel, or at least to equal the achievements of others, is implanted by nature in man's heart.

To sum up. Free competition and emulation, equality of opportunity, the natural necessity of men mutually to exchange their goods and services (to sell and buy), will result in a continuous play of demand and supply, in an unobstructed circulation of commodities. And where supply and demand or circulation of goods are continuous and unobstructed, prices will be just, i.e. proportionate to the labour and expenses. This is the natural order of exchanges; in it reigns peace and harmony. "La paix et l'équilibre ne peuvent être le résultat que de la liberté des échanges." Or, in other words, "Il n'y avait qu'à laisser faire la nature" (pp. 286, 409).

The essence of Boisguillebert's views on the supreme importance of the economic function of liberty is obviously an attack on mercantilist restrictions, which may be called the outwork of mercantilism. He then proceeds to the assault on the centre of that policy—money.

(c) *Money*.—The failure to follow the natural order could not but result in unhappiness and strife. "Les nations civilisées, en voulant substituer leur prétendue sagesse à celle de la nature, s'attirent des souffrances que ne connaissent pas les peuples barbares" (p. 386). In the age of innocence of man or during the reign of the law of nature, food and raiment were the only riches. All things that served those primary needs of man were real wealth. They could be used and enjoyed whenever they were needed. But man fell into corruption and abandoned the state of nature for that of civilization, which panders to that corruption (p. 411). He was no more satisfied with those simple necessaries, supplied to him by a few original trades—tillage, building, and tailoring—but craved for luxuries and superfluities. Trades and professions multiplied, and with them the number and variety of commodities and services demanding exchanges. Barter proved now quite insufficient to effect them, so money was invented as a medium and a pledge. Precious metals were then made into idols. The false conception and wrong employment of money caused more ravages than the barbarian invasions. Money, from being a humble servant of exchanges, was turned into a master and tyrant (pp. 395–397), who dictates which goods are to be produced, which works of industry are to be fostered, and which are to be neglected and put at a disadvantage. Money and monetary policy led to inequalities and divided society into two classes, namely, one which does no work and enjoys all the pleasures that wealth can offer, while the other is toiling from dawn till night and obtains hardly the most elementary necessaries and often nothing at all (p. 396). We may accept it as certain that nearly all crime would be banished from the State if we could banish "ce fatal métal, cette malheureuse idolaterie de l'argent, source de tous les maux" (p. 400).

Society must return to the true conception and use of money. "L'argent n'est que le gage de la tradition des biens réels. L'argent ne se bois ni se mange . . . il n'est donc pas richesse en soi." In so far as silver serves as money, it could very well be replaced by a piece of paper or parchment or even by a mere word. Wealth and poverty are always in proportion to the mass of real goods and not to the mass of money. If money is in abundance, the prices of goods rise; if money is rare, prices are low. The real goods are the valuable substance, money their measure only. It is foolish to maintain that poverty arises from money being carried out of the country; it is equally foolish to be afraid of the consequences of the exportation of money. Loss of money is only a real loss to countries like Peru (p. 349);

if their silver and gold mines were exhausted, the inhabitants would lack the means to procure for themselves the necessary commodities. But in countries which possess no mines, money is only a medium and a pledge. Its mass in circulation will always depend on demand and supply of real goods. If goods are in demand, supply will follow and money will be available (p. 349). There are but two indispensable conditions for the prosperity of a country—namely, continuous demand for goods and reciprocal exchanges according to justice. The latter is the more important, for if it is violated, all proportion between the prices of goods, all equilibrium is lost, and commerce and wealth disappear (pp. 278–279).

Boisguillebert's social and monetary are directed against mercantilist doctrine and policy. His reasoning moved in the same direction as that of his English contemporaries, Dudley North and Charles Davenant, but not always with the same motives. The Frenchman stood much nearer the Aristotelian and Scholastic teaching than the two English economists. This is most evident in his emphasizing the primacy of ethics over economics and in his conception of money. With the Englishmen, money was a commodity like any other, and not tainted with sin. They would never have asserted that civilization was synonymous with corruption; or that if money were abolished, nearly all crimes would disappear (pp. 399–400). They combated the balance of trade doctrine, because it was economically unsound. Boisguillebert fought it, because it was both ethically and economically a wrong doctrine. This is not to say that he was an abstract thinker only. We shall see in the subsequent chapter that he applied his doctrines to the condition of France in the reign of Louis XIV, and endeavoured to demonstrate that the neglect of commutative justice in the corn trade led to the economic ruin of France.

(d) *Condition of France.*—Boisguillebert's first book (*Détail de la France*) begins with a sentence which was destined to form the main tenet of physiocracy, namely, "The wealth of every country is in proportion to the fertility of its soil" (p. 171).[1] Riches or poverty are the effect of climate and soil, that is, of their fitness or unfitness for the production of those things which are necessary for life, or with which those things can be procured. An exception are Spain and Holland. The Spaniards draw their riches from American mines, the Dutch from traffic.

The best soil, unless cultivated, does not differ from the most inferior soil (p. 193).

In his second book (*Traité des Grains*) our author extends the conception of wealth by including the production of industry. The wealth of France, as of every other country, he declares, is of two kinds—the fruits of the earth and the fruits of industry, but the latter have their origin in the fruits of the earth (p. 354). There are in France about two hundred trades and professions which are thought to be indispensable to

[1] Quesnay is of the same opinion: "L'origine, le principe de toute richesse est la fertilité de la terre" (*Œuvres*, p. 533).

and characteristic of any civilized and polished nation, but they are one and all "les enfants de la terre" (p. 405). It is the fruits of the earth which set them all in motion. All the trades and professions depend for their existence on them (pp. 405–406).

The land, then, is the primary potential source of all wealth, that is, of the totality of consumable goods, for it is consumption (demand, need, utility) which gives them value and makes them into wealth (p. 281).

Now, in view of the supreme importance of cultivated land, it would be reasonable to assume that the State would, to say the least, avoid injuring tillage. For, granted the premises that the land and its fruits give birth to all necessaries and conveniences of life, the conclusion is inescapable that "if agriculture is ruined, all goes down" (p. 410).

In the reign of Henry IV and his minister Sully— our author is never tired to exalt their care for tillage— the State was always mindful of the interests of the cultivators. France prospered because the tiller of the soil prospered. But with the accession of Louis XIV (1660) agriculture was not only neglected, but injured through the trade policy and the methods of taxation. The condition of the farmer went from bad to worse; the yield of the land progressively declined, likewise consumption and the revenue of the realm, and France grew poorer and weaker in power.

That is the main burden of Boisguillebert's message. His books are the mirror of his composite character; an ardent propagandist, when he is searching for historical evidence or statistical figures to support his pleading for reform; an analytical mind, when he dispassionately inquires into certain economic categories and the general causes of social discontents. In his zeal to condemn contemporary abuses he depicts the reign of Henry IV and Sully as radiant with light, and the reign of Louis XIV and Colbert as covered with darkness. And the year "1660" (accession of Louis XIV) is black-marked again and again as the fateful date of the fall of France. It is all so clear-cut and sharply partitioned, without any curve, without any transition, and without any regard to the measures and influences which preceded "1660." We know now that the year "1660" really started in 1596, and was continued with Laffemas in 1615 by Montchrétien, in 1626 by Richelieu, and then in the development in the time of Mazarin. Furthermore, that Colbert's began in 1664 and 1667, with his protectionist tariffs. It is always suspicious when an author puts down in black and white the precise date of the beginning of a crisis. This is the weakest part—the propagandist part —of our author's works, which are in many respects of much value in the history of economic thought and of great human interest in the annals of the French people.

(e) *His Economics*.—From the preceding chapters it is fairly evident that we need not look in his works for any clear and consistent definitions of the economic categories, such as value, price, profit, interest, rent, division of labour, manufacture, commerce, etc. Political economy was, with Boisguillebert, not a science of production, distribution, and exchange of commodities; he did not inquire into the laws or rules or cost of production, nor by what laws or considerations the commodities are actually exchanged or distributed. Political economy was, with him, political justice. practical ethics, which should teach us how to secure social harmony, universal solidarity and equilibrium, in short to allow the law of nature to function. He was pre-eminently a Catholic moral philosopher, differing only from the Schoolmen by his emphasis on free competition as the best regulator of the just price, instead of fixing statutory prices; though he pleads also, like the Schoolmen before him and the physiocrats after him, for a strong central authority to protect the tiller of the soil from the cupidity of the merchant (pp. 355–356). With Boisguillebert, ethics has the primacy over economics and politics: if exchanges are reciprocal, if the commercial scales are equal the natural harmony of interests will secure prosperity as the reward of the labour of man. Justice has, above all, to be applied to the exchanges of the tiller of the soil, for on his prosperity depends the well-being of all other trades and professions.

The obstacles in the way to safeguarding justice are the mercantilist restrictions on exchanges (particularly on the corn trade) and the avidity of the merchant to take advantage of the agricultural population. It is against those evils that our author is fighting. The restrictions on the corn trade kept the price low. In 1660 a setier (about twelve bushels) of corn was sold at ten or eleven livres. In 1700 and the following years, "in which we are," the price of corn is about the same, while all other commodities doubled in price in consequence of the influx of gold and silver from America. The State refuses to recognize these economic movements, so that the cultivator is forced to sell cheap and to buy dear. He exchanges two setiers for the price of one. Justice is violated. The tiller of the soil is being impoverished by the merchant and manufacturer. But natural law cannot be violated with impunity. The cultivator restricts his consumption, that is, his demand for commodities, so that arts and crafts, the shopkeeper and merchant, suffer a diminution of their commerce. And if consumption declines the national revenue decreases. The social equilibrium becomes unstable, all the more so as at the same time the government makes larger and larger demands on the resources of the nation.

The burden of the *taille* is heavy enough, and it is made quite unbearable by its arbitrary incidence. Some pay from 200 setiers only four, while the poor peasant pays thirty (pp. 402–403). The same arbitrariness prevails in the incidence of *aides*, which often exceed of value of the wine. The tax-farmer and the tax-collector are pocketing the larger part of the direct and indirect taxes. The "détail et factum de la France" is now this: first, the farmer has been deprived not only of the capital necessary for the cultivation and improvement of his land, but even of the ability to defray the expenses of tillage; secondly, the king's taxes cannot be levied but by imprisonments of his subjects or distraints upon their chattel. Yet there is no lack of money in the country, but much of it is hoarded. Nor is there any lack of fertile land, but much of it is laid fallow.

Much injury was also caused by high tariffs: "les douanes sont aussi funestes que les aides." The customs duties banished the merchant stranger from our ports (p. 203 *et seq.*), and, worse still, they involved us in conflicts and wars with our neighbours.

Those are the fatal results of the violation of the law of nature, of justice and equity in the exchange of goods among individuals, provinces, and kingdoms.

More police, more regulations, and edicts will not remedy or remove the evils arising from injustice. Only "le retour aux lois de la justice et de la raison retablirait l'harmonie sociale." This is the final sentence of his *Dissertation sur les richesses*.[1]

In practice this meant: (1) Freedom of trade, both internal and foreign; (2) abolition of tax-farming; (3) establishment of public revenue authorities; (4) equalization of the incidence of the *taille*; (5) reduction of the *aides*.

[1] Literature: J. E. Horn, *L'Économie Politique avant les Physiocrats*, Paris, 1867; F. Cadet, *Boisguillebert, Precurseur des Économistes*, Paris, 1870; Hazell Roberts, *Boisguillebert*, New York, 1925, the latter is best for biographical data of Boisguillebert.

V

FRANCOIS QUESNAY

1. Influences on the Formation of His Views

A half-century intervened between the publication of Bosguillebert's final work (*Factum de la France*, 1707) and Quesnay's first physiocratic paper "Fermiers," in D'Alembert's and Diderot's *Encyclopédie* (1756). In those five decades, which witnessed the collapse of the grand monarch's policy and John Law's financial schemes, the idea of the "return to nature" or escape from a civilization the bases of which were manufacture, traffic, and finance, gained entrance into many thinking minds of France.

Civilization, as it had developed ever since early modern times, with its scientific discoveries, revival of art, and mercantilist economies, gave rise to doubts and misgivings. It grew into a problem. Has man really grown wiser and more virtuous than he was in the "dark" ages? This question was put in 1749 by the academy of Dijon, which set out a prize for an essay in answer to it: "Si le rétablissement des sciences et des arts a contribué a épurer les mœurs?" The prize-winner was, as it is well known, Jean-Jacques Rousseau, who answered the question in the negative sense, that is, in accordance with the Stoic and medieval conception of the law of nature. Civilization, with its harmful and "vaines connaissances," leads to dissolution, unhappiness, and corruption. The primitive tribes, as Tacitus teaches, were happier, and there was more virtue in them than in the civilized communities. The blissful state of man is to be achieved by accepting "ignorance, innocence, and poverty," instead of searching for "lumières et funestes arts."[1] This is the final sentence of the prize essay. Its essence is quite in conformity with Catholic sentiment and with Bois-guillebert's *Dissertation sur les richesses.*

The essay took Paris by storm. On the morning of its publication, Rousseau woke up a famous man. He had expressed the sentiments of the many, for in those years "there was not a single thinker who did not fling a stone at society as it existed."[2] In 1751 D'Alembert and Diderot started the publication of the *Encyclopédie.* In 1753 Rousseau published his *Discours sur l'origine de l'inégalité,* pointing to the fateful first enclosure of a piece of land of the common earth as the beginning of inequality. Two years later came a full code of the laws of nature (*Code de la nature,* 1755), written by Morelly, and demonstrating how Nature in her wisdom implanted in man the physical propensities, appetites, and faculties which, but for the neglect of their meaning and their perversion by man, could have given rise

[1] "Dieu tout-puissant, Toi qui tiens dans tes mains les esprits, delivres-nous des lumières et des funestes arts, et rends-nous l'ignorance, l'innocence et la pauvreté, les seuls biens, qui puissnt faire notre bonheur."—Rousseau, *Discours sur les sciences et arts,* ed. 1819, p. 44 (*Œuvres,* vol. i). It reads like the prayer of a saintly minorite.

[2] E. Daire, *Les Physiocrates,* Introduction, p. vii.

to a harmonious social order, leading to happiness and virtue.

In this atmosphere, which stimulated the imagination to construct a dazzling future or to idealize the past and far distant lands, Quesnay put aside his life-long medical researches and took to economics. Trained in the observation of phenomena, he was not satisfied with generalities, but inquired into the economic life of his people. No doubt the laws of nature were violated and the *ordre naturel* was neglected, but all those errors left us still in the dark as to the particular causes and effects, that is, the decay of agriculture, the inordinate spread of traffic and manufacture of artificial commodities, the adoration of money, and the deplorable exiguity of the national revenue.

That those questions suggested themselves to him was due to the influences of his upbringing, the rural environment in which he lived till the age of forty, finally, to his study of ancient and medieval thought as well as contemporary economics tracts, though in his physiocratic writings there are few direct references to other authors or quotations from them. The only ancient writers he mentions are Xenophon and Cicero; of non-French authors he refers only to Locke and Cantillon.

2. *Biographical Data*

François Quesnay was born in 1694. The year of his birth is the only undisputed statement that can be made about his younger years. For neither the statements concerning his native place, nor the status of his parents, nor his pre-academic education are free from contradiction. Some sources give Mérey, a village near Montfort l'Amaury, as his native place, others refer to Ecqueville. Some make his father an *avocat*, busy in his profession at Montfort; others make him a small farmer. Some relate that his mother was intellectually alert and influenced her son's education; others that she was an ignorant woman and against all book-learning. There is, however, the undisputed statement that François was illiterate till the age of eleven. From this we may infer that it is not likely that his father belonged to the professional classes, for a man in this position could not possibly have kept his son for so many years without any schooling. On the other hand, a poor peasant family could not help keeping their boy to some sort of work in the farm-house, assisting his parents during the spring and summer, or minding cattle, until somebody, perhaps a benevolent nobleman or the *curé*, discovered the highly gifted peasant boy and gave him an education.

The first book he read was *La Maison rustique*, a description of village life and its husbandry. He then learned Latin and Greek—"presque sans maître" according to his admirers and friends,[1] and he used often to walk to Paris to buy second-hand copies of Plato, Aristotle, and Cicero. I should not be surprised

[1] Quesnay, *Œuvres*, pp. 18, 41.

to learn that he acquired also some volumes of St. Thomas Aquinas, for, as will be seen later on, he was well versed in philosophy and theology. There is in his writings, as said above, no reference to the Schoolmen, but Quesnay's intimate friend and best popularizer, Le Mercier de la Rivière, quotes Aristotle and Aquinas.[1]

Having thus acquired some learning in the humanities and logic, Quesnay had to decide on his future career. After some hesitation—I surmise that he hesitated between theology and medicine—he decided for the study of medicine, and left his native village for Paris, pursuing successfully his studies for several years and finally obtained his licence. He then established himself as a village physician, mainly at Mantes, an agricultural and wine-growing district. He published several treatises and books dealing extensively with medical subjects as well as philosophical problems, which spread his fame among his colleagues and scholars. He was elected a member of the Académie des Sciences in Paris, the Royal Society in London, and other learned societies.

In 1749 he was appointed physician to the Marquise de Pompadour, and later on physician in ordinary to King Louis XV. He lived in Versailles for nearly a quarter of a century, that is, till shortly before his death in 1774, but he never became a courtier nor

[1] Le Mercier, *L'Ordre naturel*, ed. 1910, p. 331, footnote 3, "B Thomas, 2.2." B. Thomas is of course a printer's error for St. Thomas, as it is evident from the further reference to "2.2" (Secunda Secundae).

even reconciled himself to urban civilization. Medicine was his profession, but agriculture the vocation of his heart, and he was always in mental contact with the village, of whose economy he had acquired expert knowledge, as may be seen from his essays "Fermiers" and "Grains" in D'Alembert's and Diderot's *Encyclopédie*. He loved the French peasantry, and disliked the purse-proud *bourgeoisie*. He remained a rustic all his life, shy and ill at ease with royalty, though he saw them often enough in their nakedness.

Madame de Hausset (lady-in-waiting to the Pompadour), with whom Quesnay used to chat about country life and the flora of her native village, relates in her *Mémoires* some characteristic incidents about his relation to the Court of Versailles. Having noticed his embarrassment when in the presence of the king, she asked him the reason of it. He gave her the following explanation: "I left the village at the age of forty, and I have little experience of the world, and it is hard for me to get used to it. When I am in the presence of the king, I say to myself: 'Voilà un homme qui peut me faire couper la tête.' " Madame de Hausset demurred by pointing to the high sense of justice of the king, whereupon Quesnay replied: "Cela est bon pour le raisonnement, mais le sentiment est plus prompt."[1]

Quesnay was steadfast in his Christian faith, the tenets of which he held to be beyond space and time. In a polemic against the mystical pantheism of Male-

[1] Quesnay, *Œuvres*, p. 132 *passim*, where many excerpts from Hausset's *Mémoires* are reproduced.

branche, he declared that all attempts to penetrate the mysteries of religion were fruitless. The incomprehensible could not be made comprehensible. It was beyond the power of reason to "vaincre une ignorance à laquelle il faut se soumettre nécessairement."[1] In one of his disquisitions, he deals also with the immortality of the soul, and with reward and punishment hereafter. He did not intend to philosophize, for he was "sufficiently instructed about those truths through revelation."[2] His purpose was only to demonstrate that all human knowledge was in perfect conformity with the dogmas of faith.

3. *Literary Work*

Quesnay wrote extensively on medicine and surgery; his most important work is *Essai physique sur l'économie animale* (final edition in three large volumes, 1748), in which he deals also with the philosophical problems mentioned above. Those books he published under his name. On the other hand, his physiocratic papers and articles appeared anonymously or under

[1] Quesnay, *Œuvres*, pp. 746, 758-763.
[2] Compare this simple confession of faith with the following: "La raison humaine est si peu capable de démontrer par elle même l'immortalité de l'âme que la religion a été obligée de la nous révéler." The latter is a quotation from Voltaire (*Œuvres*, 1825, vol. 69, p. 108). Quesnay said something similar, yet what a difference! It is the difference which Goethe expresses when he makes Margaret naïvely reply to Faust's confession of faith: "This is all good and right, the priest says much the same, but in words somewhat different . . . yet must it be unsafe; thou art no Christian."

a pseudonym in various periodicals (Mirabeau's *L'Ami des Hommes*, Dupont's *Journal de L'Agriculture*, Baudeau's *Ephémérides du Citoyen*). His first economic essays, "Fermiers" and "Grains" were written for the famous *Encyclopédie* (1756–1757); they bear the impress of Boisguillebert's critical outlook on the condition of France, and cannot be characterized as strictly physiocratic.

Quesnay is best known by the *Tableau Œconomique* (this was the original spelling) which he wrote for King Louis XV at the end of 1758. Of this edition no copy is extant. It was reprinted in 1759. A facsimile of the proofs, either of the original edition or of the second, was made by the British Economic Association (Royal Economic Society) in 1894 (British Museum Catalogue, press mark R.Ac. 2359b). It is a tract of twelve quarto pages, with marginal corrections, found in the Mirabeau collection of the Paris Bibliothèque Nationale by Stephen Bauer. An "Explication" of the *Tableau* was given by Mirabeau in 1760, and reprints of the *Tableau Économique*, with various modifications of the original, were inserted by Mirabeau in his *Philosophie rurale* (1763, 1766). An English translation of the essential parts of Mirabeau's book which concern the *Tableau* appeared in London in 1766. The final formulation of the Tableau was published by Quesnay in 1766 in the *Journal de l'Agriculture, du Commerce, et des Finances*, and reproduced by Dupont in his *Physiocratie* (1767). The main difference between the final and the original sketch of the *Tableau* is that in the original the paradigm is a single farm and a single workshop, with respective circulating capitals (*avances annuelles*) of 600 or 300 livres, while in the final edition the whole economy of a realm is treated, with proportionately larger production; in the latter agriculture disposes of ten milliards fixed capital, and an annual outlay or circulating capital of two milliards, while to arts and crafts (manufacture) no fixed capital is assigned, but only a circulating capital of one milliard. The main theme is the annual distribution and circulation of the output of agriculture and manufactures which are represented by a diagram. We deal with the essentials and obscurities of the *Tableau* in a later chapter.

Dupont was the first writer who collected some of Quesnay's articles and essays, together with the *Tableau*, and published them in 1767 in his *Physiocratie*, prefacing the book with a long introduction. The second economic writer who reproduced Dupont's collection and added to it Quesnay's essays in the *Encyclopédie*, was Eugène Daire in *Les Physiocrates*, Paris, 1846. The best, because complete, collection of Quesnay's writings was edited and published by August Oncken in 1888 under the title *Œuvres Économiques et Philosophiques*. It is a volume of eight hundred closely printed pages, large octavo, and it contains also the eulogistic addresses delivered by the friends and admirers of Quesnay after his death; Oncken included also excerpts from Madame de Hausset's reminiscences of Quesnay, as mentioned above. These additions alone take up one hundred and forty pages. Quesnay's largest paper (over hundred pages) deals with the agrarian constitution of China (*Despotisme de la Chine*), which its author treats as a model of what a social order should be; he was most pleased to find that in China the cultivator of the soil stood in the public estimation above the merchant and the manufacturer. Oncken's edition has the great merit of completeness; his footnotes are also serviceable, but his bulky and "weighty" volume has neither an index nor those short synopses of contents which E. Daire put at the head of each chapter of the economic works edited by him in 1843 and 1846, and which make them so readable.[1]

4. *Comparison with Boisguillebert and Adam Smith*

Quesnay's ideas, disseminated, reiterated, and reasoned upon in essays, articles, and dialogues, and compressed in his *Tableau Économique*, may be divided into two parts—one critical and the other positive. He is critical and increasingly condemnatory of mercantilist doctrine and policy. All criticism which deserves this appellation and which influences man's thought, presupposes some positive and constructive viewpoint from which the object of criticism is examined and tested. What is the positive and constructive aspect of Quesnay's work? And what is his

[1] All references, also those in brackets, are to A. Oncken's edition of Quesnay's *Œuvres*, 1888.

standing in the history of economics? These questions
touch our main problem: What is the meaning of
physiocracy? For there was no other exponent of that
system but Quesnay. All the other adherents of the
physiocratic school, such as Mirabeau the elder,
Dupont de Nemours, Le Mercier de la Rivière, Abbé
Baudeau, Le Trosne, are no more than his popu-
larizers, as far as each of them understood their master.

A comparison of Quesnay with Boisguillebert and
Adam Smith may suggest some answer to our questions.

Boisguillebert, who started from the same economic
principle as Quesnay—namely, that "agriculture is
the only source of riches"—was, like him, critical of
mercantilist views and policies, but the bulk of his
writings is directed against the financial measures of
Louis XIV. His criticism led to the proposal of certain
reforms: freedom of trade and equity in taxation—
intended to make the prevailing order more satisfactory. As a scholar, as a practical business man, and
a high official and nobleman, his position was closely
bound up with the conditions of France in the reign
of Louis XIV. He was a part of it. Quesnay, on the
other hand, was mainly a scholar, a trained observer,
sentimentally a peasant, utterly out of sympathy with
the existing economic order. He was thus much less
bound up with the prevailing social conditions and he
went much farther in his criticism as well as in his
constructive proposals than did his predecessor. He
desired to establish an *ordre naturel* in the place of the
existing order, which he regarded as artificial and

unsound, morally and materially wrong. *"Établissement de l'ordre naturel et essentiel"*—thus formulates Le Mercier the aim of physiocracy.[1] This work was much more difficult than that of Boisguillebert.

Adam Smith has this in common with Boisguillebert and Quesnay, that the object of his criticism was likewise mercantilism, and that he likewise pleaded for natural liberty, for freedom of trade, for free competition, but he was in a much more favourable position than Quesnay, for there was no real need for Adam Smith to construct and establish a new order. He saw it growing before his eyes; it was only necessary to remove the restraints and the obstacles that impeded the development of the new order. His *Wealth of Nations* was devoted to a demonstration of how this new order of economic life was working and to an inquiry into its methods, its causation, its laws, and how the knowledge of them could promote its growth. The state of nature was for him a phase of an irretrievable past. It was good as long as it lasted, but is now gone for ever. His mental freedom from reactions to the past, undoubtedly promoted by his deism, rationalist view of religion, and optimistic moral philosophy, and by his more progressive and prosperous environment, attached him to the growing new forces and form of industrial life.

Quite different was the spiritual and material condition of Quesnay. He was a devout Catholic, attached in perfect humility to his faith and its tenets.

[1] Le Mercier, *L'Ordre naturel*, 1910, p. 329.

A rustic by sentiment, with his heart in the village, he looked upon trade and commerce with distrust, which was strengthened by his theological and scholastic conceptions. Quesnay speaks with contempt of the "citadin," who, he thought, lived parasitically on the labour of the cultivator (p. 345). His memory was still occupied with the catastrophes of the reign of Louis XIV and the Regency; and his imagination was captivated by the state of nature, by utopian descriptions of past civilizations (Incas in Peru)[1] or by the idealization of imperfectly known distant lands ("Despotisme de la Chine"). His mind turned from the present towards the medieval past. Many of the elements of his *Ordre naturel* he found in the social doctrines of the Middle Ages. Physiocracy is, indeed, a rationalization of medieval economic life. The *Tableau Économique* is the graphic representation of that life, and not at all of the conditions of France in the eighteenth century. Only the critical aspect of Quesnay's work is applied to France of his time. Its positive and constructive aspect is modelled on medieval conditions in general.

5. *Social Principles*

Quesnay's principles and reasonings are pervaded throughout by the teachings of *ius naturale*. They are

[1] On the social constitution of the Incas in ancient Peru, Quesnay writes (*Œuvres*, p. 555): "Cet ordre était si conformé à l'ordre de la nature même, qu'il surpasse toutes les spéculations des philosophes et savants legislateurs de l'antiquité."

his guide and major premise; they are always at the
back of his mind. Numerous are the passages in his
writings which deal with the law of nature or *droit
naturel*, and with allusions to it (pp. 359–366, 373–375,
637, 641, 802–804). His style, generally restrained
and with a sober logic, grows rhetorical, prolix, and
vague whenever he is pointing to the sublimity and
supreme importance of the natural rights of man in
society. They are *irrefragable* and *immuable*, an integral part of the eternal order of the universe, where
everything is foreseen and arranged by the infinite
wisdom of the author of the world. Man can no more
create laws than he can create himself. He is only the
bearer of the laws, not their author. Rightly do we
speak, therefore, of legislators—bearers of laws—and
not of legisfactors. Those laws are made evident by
the light (*lumières*) of trained or right reason, and are
obligatory on Man (pp. 641, 802).

For all the emphasis which Quesnay put on those
laws and the numerous pages he devoted to them in
his writings, he failed to give a coherent treatment or
a consecutive exposition of their contents. It seems
that he was so saturated with the philosophy of *ius
naturale* that he either considered it a work of super-
erogation to treat its essentials in an orderly manner,
or he presupposed in his readers a knowledge thereof.
From the many scattered remarks and reflections on
those laws it is, however, not difficult to discover that
he adhered, in nearly all particulars, to the teaching of
Aquinas and Locke.

Quesnay divides the laws of nature into two categories—physical and moral. With regard to the former, his reasonings can be traced back mainly to Locke.

Man is born free and equal. Liberty is the sacred right of man. Equality is a part of the rights of man. By virtue of his instinct of self-preservation, he has a natural right to subsistence, that is, to all those things that are adapted to his use; in Quesnay's own words: "Le droit naturel de l'homme peut être défini vaguement le droit que l'homme a aux choses propres à sa jouissance" (p. 359; similarly p. 754). By what right can he make them his property, that is, exclude others from using them? The answer is, nature has endowed man with capacities to think and to work; those capacities are his personal property. He applies them to the materials supplied by nature, and by uniting his personal property (thought and labour) with the materials of nature he makes the produce his movable property, or, if he applies his work to the land, the latter becomes his "propriété foncière" (803) which nobody has a right to violate.

With regard to property, Quesnay is by no means as absolute as his commentator, Le Mercier de la Rivière. The latter, a student of Roman law and a government official, lays down the principle that the foundation of society is the right of property, "parce que sans le droit de propriété la société n'aurait aucune consistence" (*L'Ordre naturel*, ed. 1910, pp. 121–123, 337). Quesnay, however, as mentioned above, regarded the social constitution of the Incas in Peru as thoroughly sound and in perfect conformity to the laws of nature, though "les terres n'étaint point des biens possédés en propriété" (*Œuvres*, p. 555). Quesnay cared more for the prosperity of the cultivator, and aimed at securing him the means to improve agriculture and a just price for his produce.

The natural rights of man included also equality. How, then, did inequality arise? What reason is there for the unequal distribution of things or the unequal degree of liberties and rights among men in society? This is partly due—Quesnay follows here the reasonings of Locke—to man's own doings and to the inequality of abilities among men, but mainly—and Quesnay follows here Christian theology—to the designs of the supreme Intelligence who constructed the world. Man is only a small part of the universe; his sufferings and inequalities, comprised in distributive justice, serve the vast purpose of the conservation of the whole (p. 757).

So much for the physical laws of nature.

What constitutes the second category, that is, the moral category of the laws of nature? Quesnay could find in Locke no answer to that question, for the latter was a mercantilist, adhering to the balance of trade or to unequal exchanges between nations, and to the doctrine that traffic brought riches, that is, coin and bullion, to his country.[1] It was precisely that doctrine against which the teaching of physiocracy was relentlessly directed. In point of the moral laws of *ius*

---

[1] See the author's *Early British Economics*, pp. 155–156, 235.

naturale, Quesnay could only go to Aquinas and Aristotle. He fully concurred in their conceptions of the natural occupation of man (agriculture), of real wealth (objects of general demand for use), and above all, of equality of exchanges (commutative justice) and the universal solidarity of mankind. The adverse opinions formed by Quesnay of the economic system of his time were one and all due to his view that the moral laws of *ius naturale* were violated or disregarded.

We may sum up this chapter by saying that, as regards the individual man, Quesnay was with Locke —a modern moral philosopher—but as regards to the social man, that is, to the economics and government of society, he was with Aquinas—a medieval theologian —a Schoolman.

VI

QUESNAY'S ECONOMICS

1. *Productive and Unproductive Labour*

The antique and medieval man, whenever he gave thought to domestic or State economy, had no doubt in his mind that all those things that are necessary for sustenance were obtained by tillage, live-stock breeding, fishing, and hunting. These were the natural sources of real wealth. Moreover, they did not only supply the necessaries of life, but were capable also of producing a surplus, above and beyond his immediate demand and above and beyond the labour and expenses spent on their production. They were capable of producing an increase of wealth, or, in other words, they were the means to obtain riches. It was patent to all that the harvest could yield a multiple of the seed, that live-stock and poultry increased by natural instinct, as did the fishes in the lakes and seas, the deer and wild-fowl in the woods. They were the natural sources of sustenance and riches, and the occupations concerned with them were natural occupations. This, as we already know from a former chapter, was the settled opinion of Socrates and Aristotle, and summed up by Cicero, who declared: "Omnium autem rerum ex quibus aliquid acquiritur, nihil est agricultura melius, nihil uberius . . ." (*de Officiis*, book i, 151). Of all the means to acquire wealth none is better and none is more profitable than agriculture.

The surplus, which those natural occupations yielded, was exchanged for goods of which there was a deficiency, or for money—a measure of value and a pledge that the goods that were needed would be available when the occasion for them arose. This operation constituted commerce—a commutation of goods, which was likewise natural.

Failing or disregarding those natural sources, either from the niggardliness of the physical environment or from human motives or vicissitudes, man made it his business to traffic or to lend money on usury in order to obtain riches. These occupations are unnatural, that is, not in consonance with the law of nature. This is the opinion of Aristotle, the Fathers, and the Schoolmen.

Arts and crafts, or manufacture, likewise produce wealth (that is, objects for the use and enjoyment of man), but do not increase it. They produce no surplus above the labour and expense laid out on their production.[1] They yield no profit, no riches, but merely transform or "consume" natural materials, natural wealth, by giving them a different shape. They are useful, but unproductive of new riches. This was the view of the antique and medieval man.

Landowners, cattle breeders, foreign merchants (traffickers), money-lenders, and money-changers could respectively acquire riches in a natural or unnatural

[1] See the author's *Early British Economics*, p. 230.

way, but craftsmen, workpeople, and manufacturers could only earn their sustenance, since the goods they produced amounted to no more than a change of their labour and expenses from one form into another.

The physiocratic idea of the unproductivity of manufcturing work is apt to strike us as paradoxical. Familiar as we have grown with Smith-Ricardian and socialist economics concerning labour as the source of value and surplus value or profit, we are inclined to assume that any other conception of productive labour cannot be but the result of some fallacy. We fail, however, to consider that the view of productive or unproductive labour depends on the prevailing conception of wealth. A generation or an age or a school which regards "natural" occupations as the only ones that are productive of wealth, cannot think of "artificial" commodities as enriching the life of the people, just as the mercantilist age which regards money (coin and bullion) as wealth *par excellence*, cannot think of occupations as productive which fail to bring money into the country. We shall presently see that as soon as the concept of wealth broadens and includes all sorts of material commodities, all labour is considered as productive which adds value to commodities, while the occupations of the men of letters, scientists, physicians, etc., are classed as unproductive, because spiritual values are not regarded as wealth.

From the break-up of the Middle Ages (or from the

first quarter of the sixteenth century) till the last quarter of the seventeenth century—the period in which English mercantilism flourished—economic writers and statesmen regarded those occupations only as productive of additional wealth, which brought in cash and bullion from abroad. The source of profit was not the factory, but the foreign market, which was to be manipulated by the balance of trade policy. John Hales, Thomas Mun, Edward Misselden, Francis Bacon, and Lewes Roberts knew quite well that skilled labour added a multiple of value to the raw material, but it only became productive through traffic. More-over, if the commodities wrought by skilled labour were not exported, they were regarded as unproductive, whatever the amount of value which labour added.

The author of *A Discourse of the Commonweal of this Realm of England* (1549), the treatise ascribed to John Hales, and with which English political economy starts on its career, divides the trades or "misteries" into three classes. "Some, like mercers, haberdashers, etc. doe fetch out our treasure of the country," and therefore are injurious rather than beneficial. The second class consists of tailors, shoemakers, carpenters, etc., who get their living in the country; they are useful, but not productive, they do not enrich the country. The third class consists of clothiers, tanners, cappers, glovers, papermakers, silver and goldsmiths, needlemakers, etc., who must be cherished, for their occupations are productive of riches, for they work for export.[1] Thomas Mun, the famous author of *England's Treasure by Foreign Trade*, writes: "We know that our natural wares doe not yield us so much profit as our industry. For iron ore in the mines is of no great worth, when it is compared with the advantage it yields . . . being cast into ordnance, muskets, etc." None the less he is strongly convinced that home trade is unproductive and that "the ordinary means to increase our wealth and treasure is by foreign trade."[2] The identical views are expressed by Francis Bacon (*Essays*, XV). The sum and substance of those views are given by Lewes Roberts: "The earth and artificial commodities are the true sources of wealth." The efficiency, skill, ability of the workmen "give true credit to the fabrics and works. But even the earth and labour wouldn't enrich a country without traffic."[3]

In the last quarter of the seventeenth century, when manufacturing progress and its new economics of production were undermining the balance of trade doctrine, and money came to be regarded as a commodity like any other commodity which formed a unit of wealth, the author of *Britannia Languens* initiated a new classification of productive and unproductive labour. He declares that it is the artificers, the "mechanick fellows," who increase the wealth of the nation, while the clergy, the liberal professions, and the shopkeepers are unproductive: "If 100,000 manufacturers get £6

[1] *A Discourse of the Commonweal*, ed. 1893, pp. 64, 91–92.

[2] Thomas Mun, *England's Treasure*, chaps. 2 and 3, par. 12.

[3] Lewes Roberts, "Treasure of Traffic," 1641, p. 9, in McCulloch's *Early Economic Tracts*.

per annum apiece, the nation must gain or save £600,000 per annum by their labour, supposing the materials be meliorated only by the value of their wages."[1]

This classification of occupations was adopted by Adam Smith, who declares: "There is one sort of labour which adds to the value of the subject upon which it is bestowed; there is another which has no such effect. The former, as it produces value, may be called productive, the latter unproductive labour." In the class of unproductive professions "must be ranked . . . churchmen, lawyers, men of letters of all kinds."[2]

When a new generation, as I ardently hope, will broaden the concept of wealth by including spiritual values a re-classification of labour will take place, so that which Adam Smith classified as unproductive will top the list of the productive labour of man.

2. *Agriculture and Manufacture*

Quesnay's economic principles are: "La terre est l'unique source des richesses, et c'est l'agriculture qui les multiplie" (pp. 331, 337). "L'origine, le principe de toute dépense et de toute richesse est la fertilité de la terre" (p. 553). The earth and its fertility are the only source of riches, and they increase through cultivation.

Riches are those consumable things which are used for the satisfaction of human needs. It is the need, the

---

[1] *Britannia Languens* (1680), pp. 300–302, 357, "manufacturer" meant in those times a craftsman employed in a manufactory.

[2] Adam Smith, *Wealth of Nations*, book ii, chap. 3, beginning.

demand, or utility which makes things into "valeurs
réelles," or riches (p. 187).

Agriculture yields two kinds of riches—namely, the
annual revenue of the proprietors (the king, nobility,
and other landlords) and the returns of the labour and
expenses of the cultivators. The revenue of the proprietors is the *produit net* of the yield of the land and
its cultivation, that is, the sum which remains from
the total yield of the land after the cultivators have
deducted the cost of tillage.

The *produit net* and the cultivators' returns are the
measure and limit of the annual income of the nation;
they are the annual fund, from which all expenditure,
individual and national, are defrayed (p. 533). This
annual fund or the annual riches of the nation consists
of the total proceeds received by the cultivators from
the merchants ("de la vente de la première main")
(p. 438). The magnitude of that annual fund depends
on the price received at that sale. How is that price
determined? The price at which the cultivators offer
their produce is arrived at by taking into account their
labour and expenses as well as the surplus value which
the fertility of the soil contributes, and which is evidently estimated at the current market price. "Le prix
précède toujours les achats et les ventes" (p. 452). This
is the *bon prix*, the just price. In practice, however, it
is demand and supply that ultimately determine the
price.[1] To obtain the *bon prix*, that is, to make the

[1] "Le prix des productions est réglé par des besoins et la
quantité même des productions, qui decident de leurs valeurs

final price approach most nearly to the just price, it is indispensable that the sale should be unrestricted, for in a free market the demand will be enlarged by that of the foreign corn-dealers. Freedom of trade, unrestricted competition, will ensure the just price and the prosperity of agriculture (p. 183). In the words of Quesnay: "Laisser passer, laisser faire" (p. 671); further: "Pas trop gouverner! Ne tentez pas de fixer les prix. La concurrence seule peut régler les prix avec équité" (p. 804).

The proprietors and the cultivators are the productive class. The former, because it is their national duty to care for the land and they make the original capital outlay (*avances foncières*) necessary to prepare and ameliorate the land (clearing, drainage, etc.) for the purpose of cultivation. The cultivators are evidently the real producers. The other classes of the nation do not contribute to the increase of its riches, but merely share in its consumption. In other words, the artisans, craftsmen, professional men, merchants, and traffickers are an unproductive (sterile) class. Some sections of this class are doing useful social work, and deserve a remuneration, a salary for their labour and expense, while other sections, particularly the traffickers and the redundant tradespeople, are injurious to the welfare of the community, for it is evident that their income, which is often relatively large, is a deduction from,

vénales" (p. 534). This is the market price, while value in general is determined by the cost of production: "La valeur des productions est la consommation qu'il a fallu faire pour se les procurer" (p. 804).

and diminution of, the income of the productive class, thus crippling it in the cultivation of the soil, that is, in the production of riches (pp. 385–387). The income of the redundant tradespeople and traffickers can only arise from depressing the price of the prime materials: grain, wool, hemp, flax, wine, etc., when buying from the cultivators, that is, at the "achat de la première main." We shall return to this subject later on. Meanwhile, we have to deal with Quesnay's view of manufacture.

"Les travaux d'industrie ne multiplient pas les richesses" (pp. 233–234). "Les travaux des marchandises de main-de'œuvre et d'industrie pour l'usage de la nation ne sont qu'un objet dispendieux et non une source de revenu" (p. 343). The works of craftsmen and manufacturers do not increase the riches, but are costly objects and not a source of the revenue of the realm. The value of such commodities is in direct proportion to the value of the materials employed and the subsistence which the workers consume. They are unproductive of new wealth.[1] The labour, skill, and capital employed in the construction of buildings, machines, or in the manufacture of furniture, clothing, jewellery, etc., are merely assembling, re-uniting, and conserving the various categories of

---

[1] "La valeur vénale des marchandises de main-d'œuvre n'est que la valeur même de la matière première et de la subsistance que l'ouvrier a consommée pendant son travail" (p. 537). And Le Mercier defines price as follows: "Le prix nécessaire d'un ouvrage . . . se forme des debourses faits par l'ouvrier pour l'achat des matières premières, et du montant de toutes ses consommations pendant son travail" (L'Ordre naturel, ed. 1910, p. 312).

riches, *plus* the substance which the craftsmen consumed (p. 804). It is only the productive works which are capable not merely of defraying their own cost but also of supplying the increment of riches, which forms the revenue of the nations. "A sum of ten milliards invested in sterile employment during a period of twenty years will continue to amount to no more than ten milliards, while the same sum employed in agricultural pursuits during the same period will yield hundred and ten milliards" (p. 469). In another passage Quesnay makes the remark that "two million men employed in agriculture can produce values to the amount of one milliard, while three million men employed in arts and crafts will produce commodities of the value of seven hundred millions only" (p. 289, footnote). It is this advantage which differentiates productive from sterile occupations.

It was inevitable that the manufacturers, merchants, and their economists, mainly moderate mercantilists, such as Véron de Forbonnais, should utterly disagree with Quesnay's view that manufacture and foreign trade should be classed among the sterile occupations. We hear the echo of their complaints in Adam Smith's work (book iv, chap. 9), where it is said that the French school of economists "endeavours to degrade the artificers, manufacturers, and merchants by the humiliating appellation of the barren or unproductive class."[1] The French opponents of physiocracy, in

[1] Adam Smith forgets that he himself degraded "some of the gravest and most important . . . professions, churchmen, lawyers,

refutation of its doctrine, pointed as an instance to lace-making, where the finished product exceeded by thousands per cent the value of the raw material and the sustenance of the workers, so that the enormous increment could only have resulted from the productive labour of the lace-makers. Le Mercier de la Rivière, the commentator of Quesnay, took up the defence of the school, with the following arguments, which, leaving out several pages of rhetoric, amount to this (*L'Ordre naturel*, ed. 1910, pp. 320–325).

It was quite true that in lace-work the raw material worth 20 sols (about tenpence) yields a product worth thousand *écus* (about £100). But, if we take into account the cost of the flax, sustenance, tools, capital outlay, interest on the capital, expenses of managements, taxes, risk premium, remuneration of the entrepreneur, then the whole illusion of the increased riches is dissipated: "L'addition de tous ces divers objets réunis vous donne un total qui devient le prix necéssaire de la dentelle. . . . Les profits éblouissants de cette fabrique sont de vains phantômes . . . qui se dissipent dès que la lumière parait" (*ibid.*, p. 324).

Those expenses, quite exorbitant in relation to the cost of the prime material, had to be defrayed. And since they could not be met from the increase of value of the lace, for according to the physiocratic doctrine there was no increase of value in manufacture, they

physicians, men of letters" by ranking them among the unproductive classes, as mentioned above, p. 120.

must ultimately be a charge on the productive class. The inordinate growth of "manufacture de luxe" and arts and crafts could not but result in the decline of agriculture. The capital necessary for the improvement of the soil, raising the quality of the produce and live-stock, acquisition of better instruments of production, was withdrawn to sterile occupations. Artisans filled the towns to produce *objets de luxe* for the nobility and merchants, while the countryside suffered from the neglect of tillage,[1] which in turn reacted un-favourably on the well-being of the nation. For, "pauvres paysans, pauvre royaume" (p. 804).

There are, however, certain conditions which make manufactures beneficial and profitable. These con-ditions are:

(1) If arts and crafts and manufacture are making use of the surplus native raw materials and the appro-priate capacities and skill of the craftsmen. These factors will enable the manufacturers to produce commodities with less expense than their competitors abroad who do not enjoy those facilities. They can offer at lower prices and thus find ready sales when exported. Our exporters will then be able to buy there those goods which the other nations can produce

[1] "Les manufactures et le commerce entretenus par le désordre du luxe, accumulent les hommes et les richesses dans les grandes villes, s'opposent à l'amélioration des biens, dévastent les cam-pagnes, inspire des mépris pour l'agriculture . . . et affaiblissent l'État" (p. 189). They are also the cause of the decrease of the population, for it is the prosperity of agriculture on which the increase of the population depends: "Les hommes se multiplient à proportion des revenus des bienfonds" (p. 234)

cheaper than we. By this means the commerce among nations will be promoted to the benefit of all. Commerce will thus be reciprocal and on the basis of equality. The main injury done by manufacturers arises from their foreign materials for the production of commodities which serve the lust for *luxe*, and for which the country does not possess the necessary requirements. Capital and labour are thus withdrawn from agriculture to the injury of the nation. Besides, manufactures dependent on foreign raw materials can never successfully compete with countries where those raw materials are indigenous, and where the work-people are trained for their transformation into commodities.

(2) Manufacture may contribute to the increase of the national revenue if it employs labour which is redundant in agriculture. By this means those workmen enable the nation to make profits on the foreign market; moreover, the gainfully employed artisans would then form a home market for agricultural produce.

3. *Commerce and Traffic*

The French mercantilists, headed by Véron de Forbonnais, who opposed Quesnay, raised the objection that "la doctrine physiocratic regarde toutes les sociétés comme une seule famille, qui ne doit pas avoir des intérêts opposés" (p. 670). Quesnay, from his universalist viewpoint, looked upon mankind, with its various geographic divisions, as a single community, whose members exchanged the surplus of their goods on the basis of justice; value for value, without loss or gain to anyone, but to the benefit of each. The same natural law which governed the economic relations between man and man within one country should be applied also to trading between various countries.

Such exchanges are commerce. "Le commerce n'est qu'un échange de valeur pour valeur égale et . . . il n'y a ni perte ni gain entre les contractants" (p. 536). Both parties benefit, for each acquires for its superfluity the use and enjoyment (*jouissance*) of portions of wealth which they lacked before. As long as those exchanges take place in direct transactions between producer and consumer the principle of equality unquestionably holds good. But when the exchanges are performed through the intermediary of merchants, there is a shifting of values.

The merchant buys from the producer and sells to the consumer. He incurs expenses and expects a salary for his services which have to be defrayed. From what fund are the charges to be met? The merchant does this by raising the price. If we now consider that "commercer n'est pas produire," that is, that commerce creates no new values, no new wealth, the rise in price which the merchant effected, can only be explained by either of the two alternatives: the merchant as buyer (from the cultivators) does not pay the just price, or he as seller (to the consumer) fixes the price above the just price. In either case the charges will fall ultimately on the productive class: the latter will in the end have to defray the *faux-frais*, the fruitless expenses incurred by the merchants.[1] Generally speaking, "le commerçant tend à acheter au plus bas prix et à revendre au plus haut prix possible, afin d'étendre son bénéfice le plus possible aux dépens de la nation: son intérêt particulier et l'intérêt de la nation sont opposés" (pp. 323, 467).

This is, however, not uniformly the case. Wherever the merchant buys from the cultivators the surplus of their produce and carries it to a foreign market, he is enriching the country with the proceeds of his sale. Without the operations of the merchant the surplus produce would have lost all value.

The same consideration applies to foreign trade, carried on between nations on the basis of reciprocity. Merchants who export from the country the surplus of home production either of agriculture or manufacture, enrich the country. In a natural order, that is, where trade is unrestricted, the exchanges are always equal, and both countries benefit by mutually supplying their deficiencies. In such cases the interests of agriculture and commerce or between merchants and the nation are in harmony. Commerce of this nature is beneficial, and there is no reason why a commercial nation should be jealous of its neighbours who draw

---

[1] "Les frais du commerce sont toujours payés aux dépens des vendeurs des productions, qui jouissaient de tout le prix qu'en payent les acheteurs s'il n'y avait point de frais intermediaires. . . . Les frais peuvent, il est vrai, accroître les richesses des commerants, mais non pas celles des nations, qui les payent reciproquement" (p. 470).

from their soil and their labour a larger quantity of riches. Any intention of that nation to injure them by trade policies will likewise injure its own interests. Nations who are commercial rivals or even enemies should, none the less, maintain and, if possible, extend their economic intercourse, rather than injure one another. Reciprocal commerce is naturally maintained by the riches of vendors and purchasers, by supply and demand (pp. 239–240).

Where, however, merchants turn into traffickers (*marchands revendeurs*), then their interests and those of the nation are diametrically opposed (p. 670).

Traffic is buying, transporting, selling, importing and exporting, re-importing and re-exporting any goods which offer anywhere a chance for profit—a ceaseless process of purchases and sales, which accumulates fruitless expenses and gives rise to the expectation of salaries, which the productive classes of the nations have to meet. Even if the traffickers bring home large gains, these are not public gains. The traffickers always manage to get a share of the nation's wealth, but the nation never obtains a share in the traffickers' gains. "Le négociant est un étranger dans sa patrie" (p. 461). The traffickers form a universal mercantile republic, which draws its wealth from all nations. The small mercantile States are integral parts of that republic; they are, so to speak, its capital cities, its headquarters, its counting-houses. The mass of its money is proportionate to the extent of its commerce; it is always in reserve, ready for any profitable venture;

it never leaves the cash-box, except in order to return enhanced with increments of money. The pecuniary riches of the universal—to-day we say: international—mercantile republic cannot therefore be regarded as increasing the riches of the nations concerned. The traffickers are everywhere and nowhere at home, whatever their respective native countries may be. The scope of their profession knows neither frontiers nor particular territories. Our merchants are also the merchants of other nations, and *vice versa*, and always on the alert, always with an eye to money-getting (pp. 461, 467, 326–328). The case of the financiers is the same. A State should take care to rely, in case of extraordinary financial requirements, on its own resources, and not on financiers, since their pecuniary fortunes are clandestine riches which know "ni roi ni patrie" (p. 337). To sum up: The most advantageous policy for a State is, therefore, the continual and progressive increase of its agricultural production, and thus also of the *produit net*, and the utmost restriction of the gains of the traffickers, that is, that the payments for their services should be as low as possible. The most rational means to achieve this aim is perfect freedom of trade (pp. 669–671).

Quesnay's view of the merchant (engaged in international trade) is so utterly at variance with that of his contemporaries, *e.g.* Dean Tucker and Adam Smith, that he seems to belong to a different age. He writes in the spirit of medievalism when treating of "negotiatores." Quesnay is spiritually a contemporary of

Chaucer and John Gower, all three descend from the Schoolmen.

Chaucer, in the Prologue to the *Canterbury Tales*, introduces the merchant in the following lines (270–284):

> A Marchaunt was there. . . .
> Sownynge alway thencrees of his wynnynge.
> He wolde the see were kept for eny thinge
> Betwixe Middelburgh and Orewelle.
> Wel couthe he in eschaunge sheeldes selle . . .
> So estatly was he of his governaunce,
> With his bargaynes, and with his chevysaunce.
> For sothe he was a worthy man withalle,
> But soth to sayn, I not how men him calle.

The merchant carrying on his trade between Harwich and Middleburgh (Low Countries), is always thinking of his gains, his bargains, his profit on the exchange of coins in different markets. But the most characteristic point is that contained in the last line— Chaucer does not know the name of the merchant: "how men call him." The merchant is a stranger in his own country; his name is unknown. It is Quesnay's sentence: "Le négociant est un étranger dans sa patrie."

John Gower (*Mirour de l'Omme*, lines 25236–25244) devotes several pages to the *Triche* (fraud) of the traffickers:

> Del un Marchant au jour present
> L'en parle molt communement,
> Il ad noun Triche plein de guile,

Que pour sercher del orient
Jusques au fin del occident,
U Triche son avoir son pile.

He chastises the frauds of the universal traffickers, who deal in Bordeaux and Paris, in Florence and Venice, in Bruges and Ghent, and in "the noble city on the Thames," everywhere looking for "pile" (plunder).

4. *Money and Balance of Trade*

"L'argent considéré en lui-même est une richesse stérile qui ne produit rien" (p. 402). . . . L'argent n'a d'autre usage que de faciliter l'échange des denrées en servant de gage intermédiare entre les ventes et les achats. . . . L'Argent sert de mesure pour constater les valeurs des choses commercales" (pp. 542–543). Money (silver coins) is by itself but barren metal; it produces nothing; it serves only as a measure of value and a pledge. It measures the ratio of values of the goods which are being exchanged, and it is a pledge that the vendor who receives the money as equitable price for his goods will, as occasion arises, be able to acquire the goods he needs. Money, then, is a statutory medium of exchange.

Most people, remarks Quesnay, do, however, regard money as real riches on which the prosperity of the individual and the greatness of the State depends, for with money, they say, all things can be obtained. But they fail to ask themselves: Do we want money *per se*?

Surely not. For money as such is not serviceable for immediate use and enjoyment; it is not a consumable good; it is not true wealth. What we really desire to obtain are goods for our use and enjoyment. Those goods arise primarily from the annual yield of husbandry, and they are distributed through commerce, through mutual exchange, through commutation of various articles of merchandise by the medium of money, or coined silver.

Money, then, has its main function to render possible the exchange and distribution of goods; it is a variable quantity; the volume of available goods limits the need and mass of money in circulation. And it is also through commerce that a country, with no gold and silver mines, buys money by paying for it with goods. The production of goods, then, gives rise to commerce and to the need and possibility of obtaining money. Hence it follows that neither money not commerce, neither merchants nor traffickers bring riches, but it is, above all, the annual reproduction of the primary goods which is the source of riches and gives rise to commerce and money, procuring employment to tradespeople and merchants (pp. 324–325, 336, 289). The interests of the nations can therefore not centre on money, but on the production and mutual exchange of goods. Besides, some of the most considerable exchanges between mercantile countries are settled, not by gold and silver coins, but by pieces of paper, that is, by negotiable bills of exchange.

None the less, our statesmen have, in the last

hundred years, been directing their economic policy towards enriching the country, as they believe, by bringing in gold and silver. The contrivance they employ for achieving this purpose is the balance of trade, that is, making the exports exceed the imports. They assume that the balance of payments will be all the more favourable if the exports consist in manufactured commodities. They forget that every sale is a purchase and *vice versa*, and that both buyer and seller do not mutually exchange their goods for less than their respective value. Where freedom of trade exists, no loss or gain are possible, though both parties may benefit. Balance of payments, or inequality of exchanges, can only arise where one party is privileged through customs duties, monopoly, and other manipulations.

This is a policy which, in the end, proves both uneconomic and immoral. The promotion of manufacture by all sorts of privileges and tariff manipulations has sacrificed the interests of the tillers of the soil. The exportation of grain has been restricted in order to supply the workpeople with cheap foodstuffs. Low corn prices impoverish the farming population and lay waste large tracts of land. The injury inflicted on tillage is aggravated by the introduction of the manufacture of fancy goods and sumptuous apparel, the raw materials of which are imported from abroad, in consequence of which the demand for our home-grown raw materials has considerably decreased. The surplus of the native produce sinks to the level of *non-valeur*.

More disastrous still are the effects of the *manufacture de luxe* on the morals of the nation; the military spirit is weakened, and virtue and honour degenerate into vanity and cupidity (pp. 304, 234, 193).

The criterion of the prosperity or poverty of a country cannot be found in the balance of trade. Not what a nation exports but what it consumes at home indicates its real condition. A country may have large exports, while its people live in poverty, and conversely, the exports may be inconsiderable, not because the people are poor, but by reason of their large effective demand. A country is most prosperous when inland production and consumption are of such dimensions that there is little left and little need for foreign trade (pp. 237–239). Indeed, only nations who cannot satisfy their needs from native production must have recourse to foreign supplies. It is a makeshift, a *pis-aller*, serving either to stop some gaps in the inland economy or to get rid of some surplus which otherwise would become valueless. It is for those nations "un mal nécessaire et même indispensable" (p. 483). Furthermore, as it was shown above, accumulation of pecuniary wealth by means of foreign trade may enrich the traffickers and financiers, but the nation as a whole, far from benefiting by it, has to bear all the *faux-frais*, the useless charges which traffic incurs.

Foreign trade, as far as it is absolutely necessary, can be of use only if completely free and competition unrestricted, thus allowing the parties to negotiate on equal terms. By this means it is possible for reason to assert itself and to establish among nations some equity in exchanges.

The adherents of the balance of trade policy start from an assumption which is a negation of commercial equity. They assume that trade jealousy, conflict of interests, enmity, and a state of war are the rule among nations, each of which is endeavouring to overreach the others by stratagems and to plunder them. The consequences of that assumption are tariffs, privileges, monopolies. and finally devastating wars.

Quesnay, in an imaginary dialogue with an adherent of the balance of trade, exclaims: "Cessez, mon ami, cessez de vous égarer avec les spéculations politiques, qui cherchent à vous persuader que dans votre commerce vous pouvez profiter aux dépens des autres nations; car un Dieu juste et bon a voulu que cela fût impossible" (p. 484).

5. Rate of Interest. Taxation. Wages

Quesnay, who so vigorously advocated free competition in determining the price of goods, appeals as vigorously to governmental authority to fix the rate of interest. No liberty for the money-lender. The standard most legitimate to guide the authorities in fixing the rate of interest should be the revenue drawn from a piece of land, the value of which equals the loan-money. In other words: the revenue, which would accrue to the owner of the money if he bought with it a piece of land, is the measure of the interest on the loan he advances to the borrower. This standard is in conformity with strict justice; it causes no injury to any person, and is based on the right principle that only from the yield of tillage may a man increase his wealth.

The money-lender, dissatisfied with this rate, would argue that he could earn a larger revenue or profit by investing his money in commerce, and was therefore entitled to a higher rate of interest, but all such arguments and objections have their root in a confused and wrong conception of commerce. It has already been demonstrated that commercial profits arise from the *faux-frais*, the accumulation of futile expenses, which ultimately are a heavy charge on the productive classes, thus injuring them by diminishing the reward of their labour in tillage. The profits on commerce, themselves against the natural order, cannot therefore form a standard of the rate of interest. On the other hand, the revenue from tillage, legitimate in itself, should be the maximum standard. Within this limit an opportunity should be given to lender and borrower to settle the rate of interest, preferably below the maximum (pp. 399–406).

The problem of taxation and its incidence had loomed larger and larger in the political and economic life of France ever since the last quarter of the seventeenth century, and finally grew into a powerful contributory factor of the French Revolution. It engaged the attention of some of the keenest minds of the country, among them Boisguillebert, Vauban, Turgot,

Necker. It concerned not only the sources of taxation, but equally, if not to a higher degree, the methods of its levy and collection, particularly tax-farming, with its many abuses, financial and moral.

Quesnay, like his predecessors, saw that the various sources and methods of obtaining an adequate revenue for the government were uneconomical and vicious. The taille, aides, poll-tax, gabelle, manorial dues, etc., were but as many opportunities to the tax-farmers and collectors for arbitrariness and corruption, uniting together to oppress and impoverish the tillers of the soil and the nation as a whole. Starting from his principle that the soil was the only source of riches, and relying further on his argument that merchants, tradespeople, money-lenders, and similar middlemen would ultimately shift their expenses on to the productive classes, so that by roundabout and costly ways the proprietors of the land would bear all the burden, he proposed to abolish all the various impositions, and to make the *produit net* of agriculture the only and single source of public revenue and tithes. The recipients of the *produit net* were the proprietors of the land, who should surrender a certain percentage of their revenue to the State (p. 312) and the Church (pp. 337–338) (Le Mercier, *L'Ordre naturel*, p. 347).

The tillers of the soil, the creators of the *produit net* were exempt from all impositions; likewise the labourers, since their wages are nothing but the maintenance given to them by the farmer; to impose any tax on them would be tantamount to taxing the live-stock or the ploughs and scythes of the farmer. The latter would have to grant a rise of wages equal to the tax levied on the labourers: "L'imposition sur les hommes de travail, qui vivent de leur salaires . . . est payée par ceux qui emploient les ouvriers: de même qu'une imposition sur les chevaux qui labourent les terres, nee serait réellement qu'une imposition sur les dépenses même de la culture" (p. 338).

VII

RECAPITULATION

1 *Essentials of Quesnay's Doctrines*

The soil and its fertility, and not trade and commerce, are the source of wealth. It is obtained and increased by tillage. Wealth consists in those things which are suitable for the use and enjoyment of man. The doctrine employs uniformly the term "jouissance," and not "utilité," to define the economic concept of wealth. The term "jouissance," synonymous with "usufruit," brings us nearer to Aristotle's and Aquinas's conception of true wealth or real wealth, that is, things which satisfy in a direct manner the general human demand for food, raiment, and shelter. Wealth, in the sense of physiocratic doctrine, consists in consumable goods. It is much nearer to nature's gifts and the bodily needs of man than that which the urbanized man conceives of the substance of wealth. There is in it neither money nor luxuries. Reading and re-reading Quesnay appears to me to be the easiest method to come into intimate contact with the economics of Aristotle and the Schoolmen. He was mentally as near to them as he is in some respects, that is, with regard to liberty, near to us.

The men who produce wealth thus conceived are the only productive class in the nation. It embraces all persons employed in the production of the things which are suitable for the use and enjoyment of man. Their labours are brought to a close with the free sale of the produce "de la première main," that is, by the productive class at competitive prices, either direct to consumers, or to the sterile class—craftsmen and manufacturers, who use it as raw materials, or to corn-dealers, who supply the consumers; or, finally, to traffickers who transport the produce as merchandise to various markets for sale and re-sale.

The proceeds of these original sales (by the productive class) form the fund of values, the income, from which the nation lives and carries on its economic activities. They are the measure and limit of the annual wealth of the nation. In view of its limits and its vital importance for the existence of nation and State, constant and uninterrupted circulation, a free flow of values, is of absolute necessity. No accumulation of parts of the annual wealth in few hands should be permitted: "qu'ils ne se forment point de fortunes pécuniaires, car autrement ces fortunes pécuniaires arretraient la distribution d'une partie du revenu annuel de la nation" (p. 332). Likewise, no useless saving. The goods should freely circulate through the whole body politic. They are the life-blood, which should nowhere be obstructed or restricted in its natural course.

Distribution follows production. The producers are the first to participate in the fund. They deduct from it the cost of production (their own maintenance, wages of the labourers, repair of tools, interest on their stock, reserves for emergencies). The surplus which remains after the deductions are made is the *produit net*, which is remitted to the proprietors of the lands. A certain percentage of the *produit net* is earmarked for taxation to meet the tithes and national expenditure. This levy on the *produit net* forms the national revenue. No other taxes, direct or indirect, are to be levied on the other classes.

The unproductive class (artisans, craftsmen, manufacturers, and the various mercantile categories) lives on wages and salaries which it receives or exacts from the productive class and the proprietors of the land. It does this by raising the original price of the product. The manufacturer who bought his raw materials (flax, hemp, timber, wool, skins, or metals) from the productive class, transforms it into commodities, raises the original price to a level which free competition determines, say, by 25 or 50 per cent. This addition is no new wealth, but the cost of his labour and maintenance which he consumed during the operation; it is a replacement of the consumption of the raw materials and maintenance. The merchant who raises the original price of the produce by a percentage determined by competition, adds no new value by his handling the goods; the increase of the price is a wage for his labour. Since, however, all those operations and services do not increase the annual fund, the increase above the original price is ultimately a charge on the productive and proprietary class. The only exception is the merchant who sells the surplus produce to the consumers of neighbouring countries. He enriches his nation by the proceeds of the surplus, which but for its exportation would have lost all value.

Some members of the sterile class are performing useful, though unproductive, work, and deserve a reward of their labour. Some are useless and redundant, but all are ultimately a charge on production. The smaller, then, the number of the unproductive class, and the more its members limit themselves to the most necessary manufacturing work and commercial operations, the greater will be the ability of the productive class to improve the lands, the live-stock, and their produce, and, consequently, to increase the annual fund of wealth, and thus to enhance the *produit net* of the proprietors, to secure an adequate reward of the labour of the sterile class, to pay tithes and to replenish the national revenue.

2. *The Meaning of Physiocracy*

An attempt to subject the economic concepts of Quesnay to a critical examination would hardly be appropriate. First, because he performed this examination himself, he was fully aware of all objections that were raised or might possibly be raised against his doctrines. In his dialogues on commerce and the works of arts and crafts and manufacture (pp. 378 *et seq.*, 444–493 *passim*) he dealt, as conscientiously as any opponent would, with all arguments advanced in refutation of his views. He unreservedly admitted that his own argumentation in support of his doctrines might appear as a "raisonnement contre les faits," and none the less he maintained his position.

Secondly, no intellectual effort of any weight is required to expose the unsoundness of the economics of physiocracy, when tested by the principles of political economy or by the industrial developments which have been familiar to us ever since the latter half of the eighteenth century. Or what need is there, again, for exceptional keenness of intellect to discover the anachronism of the "autorité tutélaire" in a period of French history, when Rousseau's *Contrat Social* was captivating the thinking minds of the nation? Voltaire, who in his *L'homme à quarant écus* whetted the edge of his wit on the palpable incongruities between physiocratic doctrine and the economic conditions of the age, was only emphasizing the obvious.

We can argue to some purpose with an economic writer, who stands affirmatively in the midst of his time, accepts in the main its social structure, differing only by advancing certain theoretical views which we regard as not being in agreement with accepted opinion or logic. It is, however, quite another matter when we have to do with authors who take up a negative attitude towards their time, evidently judging it by standards of a different pattern from ours. They have in their mind, as it would seem, a different social system, which sets them into opposition to their contemporaries. We are, in fact, in the presence of economists with a social mission. In dealing with such writers, the main consideration of the critic cannot therefore be to expose the weakness of certain of their propositions, doctrines, or deductions, but to discover the outlines of their ideal system and to inquire into the causes or reasons which induced them more or less consciously to step out of their time, and either to look back to the past or constructively to imagine a future more agreeable to their views.

Adam Smith, who was for a time in personal contact with the physiocrats in Paris and who started with them from the same point—anti-mercantilism—deals with their system (*Wealth of Nations*, book iv, chap. 9), and considers it mainly as a reaction against Colbert's policy of "giving preference to the industry of the towns above that of the country." The physiocrats reversed that policy and favoured agriculture above manufacture. They acted, as Smith says, according to the proverb, "If the rod be bent too much one way, in order to make it straight, you must bend it as much to the other." This solution of the physiocratic riddle explains too much. With this "rod," bent or straight, it would be much too easy to beat down and to get rid of the difficulties that arise in philosophy, aesthetics, and economics, from the existence of two opposites: realism and nominalism, free-will and determinism, classicism and romanticism, protection and free trade. We, in our time, have witnessed the transition of Britain from free trade to protection. Can the "bent rod," or the automatic play of action and reaction, satisfactorily account for the change from the policy of Cobden and Bright to that of the Chamberlains?

Apart from that, it was shown above that the preference for agriculture was only one of the differentiating features of physiocracy. To begin with, there is the *despotisme légal* and natural liberty, *laissez-faire* and statutory interest on money; further, freedom of trade and relentless opposition to the agents of foreign trade; equality and liberty of exchanges and gross inequality of the distribution of the annual wealth, so that the nobility obtains the lion's share of the annual production. The cultivators of the soil are represented as the most precious social factor, yet they have to surrender the net yield of their tillage to another class while the labourer who assists the cultivators is put into the category of live-stock.

In the introductory chapter dealing with physiocracy as an economic problem, our attention was directed to the contradictory doctrines and discordant views which this system contains. We are now fairly prepared to see more clearly the intention and aim of Quesnay.

All the difficulties and incongruities met with in the study of physiocracy would be removed if we considered it as an attempt to rationalize medieval economic life in the light of the progress of philosophy and physical science since the sixteenth century. Quesnay, as a devout Christian and ethical economist, dissatisfied with the social life of his time and moved by the moral and intellectual influences which surrounded him (and which are referred to in a former chapter), looked back to medieval society and found it ethically more firmly based than modern society. But he also found that all medieval regulations enacted with the intention to secure commutative justice or equality of exchanges had failed of their purpose. Moreover, he found that mercantilism, using those regulations for achieving inequality of exchanges or a favourable balance of payments, did achieve its purpose. He had also learned from the physical interpretation of the law of nature that self-interest could not be suppressed, since the physical laws—according to the light of the new physical science—necessarily operated in a causative sequence. It was therefore best to allow nature and right reason to work in liberty, to remove all those commercial regulations which give to one of the parties an advantage over the other. The emphasis on liberty, or free competition as the best—because natural— regulator of prices, is the only factor which could reform medieval society into a *royaume agricole* (physiocratic state or realm) as Quesnay visualized it.

VIII

THE PHYSIOCRATIC REALM

1. *Government*

St. Thomas Aquinas teaches: "All those things that behave according to nature are best, for in everything nature operates for what is best. Now every natural government is performed by one only."[1] The universe is governed by one God; the spiritual capacities of man are moved by the brain, and the many members of his body are moved by the heart. Experience teaches that territories and cities, which are not governed by one, are subject to dissensions. Aquinas adds, however (chap. 3), that quite as much "as government by one ruler is best, so is government by a tyrant the worst."

The conception of monarchical government is put in opposition to tyrannical government. It is a Christian, medieval conception, which we find also in Shakespeare's ideal monarch, Henry V. Shakespeare, saturated as he was with medieval sentiment and thought, makes him declare:

> We are no tyrant but a Christian king,
> Unto whose grace our passion is subject,
> As are our wretches fetter'd in our prison.
> *King Henry V*, Act 1, Scene 3.

[1] "Ea quae sunt ad naturam optime se habent, in singulis enim operatur natura quod optimum est. Commune autem naturale regimen ab uno est" (St. Thomas Aquinas, *De regimine principum*, book i, chap. 2).

Quesnay is likewise of opinion that government should be centralized in a single person ("que l'autorité souveraine soît unique") who, however, should subject himself to the laws of nature. The chief of the State should be an *autorité tutélaire*, a protective sovereign, but not a *despote déprédateur*, that is, a tyrant. Government by many leads to commotions and discord. It should not be given to aristocrats or the great land-lords, for they would form a confederacy to free their lands from all taxes, reduce the labourers to abject slavery and commit the most atrocious injustice upon the people.

Nor should the government be democratic. Since the ignorance and the prejudices of the lower orders, their unbridled passions and furious outbreaks, would bring horrible disasters upon the country. Not better is a mixed government, that is, a monarchy supported by the various orders of the realm. Such a government could never work in harmony, for it would inevitably lead to endless party strife and discord, as each party would attempt to favour its own interests at the expense of the other orders. Moreover, the parties would earlier or later deprive the monarch of all his power.

Likewise to be avoided is a government of the third estate, that is, of tradespeople, craftsmen, manu-facturers, and merchants. They would soon try to obtain monopolies for their trading companies, and to oppress the farmers, whom they treat with contempt, and would compel them to sell their produce at the lowest price and then carry it away or sell it at the

highest price. Besides, the merchants with their privi-
ledged traffic, in trying to get the better of the merchants of the neighbouring countries, would cause
endless conflicts and wars with them.

The best form of government is therefore a single
authority, vested with sovereign power, but acting in
conformity with the laws of nature and the positive
laws derived from them (pp. 329–331, 637–639). To
constitute such a government it is necessary to instruct
the people in the physical and moral laws of nature.
This is the indispensable condition of good government and economic prosperity of the realm. Production,
distribution, and exchange will thus proceed according
to natural justice.

The *Tableau Économique* illustrates the economy of
the physiocratic realm.

2. *The* Tableau Économique

(a) *The Social Constitution of the Physiocratic
Realm.*—The famous *Tableau Économique* is, in its
final shape (1766), the physiocratic realm in figures. Its
author presupposes a realm, headed by a single ruler, a
personal monarch, who, as said above, is assisted by a
small number of councillors, law of nature jurists, who
should interpret the physical and moral laws inherent
in nature. The constitution of the realm is the *ordre
naturel*, agriculture forming the basis of social life and
carried on with the purpose of securing prosperity to
the cultivators of the soil and through them to the whole

realm. It numbers thirty million inhabitants, who are divided into three classes: the productive class, the proprietors, and the sterile class.

(1) The productive class (hereinafter called the producers), about half of the population, consists of the cultivators of the soil—farmers or tenants. They extract the wealth from the soil, and their labour increases the wealth. The buildings (dwellings, stables, threshing-floors, granaries, magazines), the live-stock (oxen, cows, horses, sheep, pigs, poultry), the implements (vehicles, ploughs, etc.), are the fixed capital (*avances primitives*) of the producers, representing a total value of ten milliard livres. The annual circulating capital (*avances annuelles*) of the producers (seeds, subsistence of the farmers, labourers and their families, upkeep of live-stock and of the implements), or the annual cost of production amounts to the value of two milliards. The fixed and circulating capitals exist only in kind. The pecuniary resources will be shown later.

(2) The class of proprietors or landowners, numbering less than a quarter of the population, consists of the king, his Court, the nobility, the clergy, and other landowning members of the realm. According to Le Mercier, the king is the co-proprietor of the net produce of the land.[1] Though the proprietors are socially separated from the productive class, and though their income or revenue has its only source in the annual tribute paid to them by the productive class, Quesnay regards them as productive, for by the law of nature

[1] Le Mercier, *L'Ordre naturel*, pp. 158 *et seq.*

they are charged with the care of the soil: "Les propriétaires sont de droit naturel chargés des soins de la
régie des dépenses pour les réparations de leur patri-
moine, ils ne peuvent pas être confondus avec la classe
stérile" (p. 318). Moreover, the proprietors made
originally the *avances foncières*: they bore the cost of
clearing the lands and making them fit for cultivation.
The tribute which they receive annually from the
producers consists of the whole net surplus (*produit
net*) of agricultural production. Of this net surplus the
proprietors retain four-sevenths for their own use, two-
sevenths are paid as single tax to meet the expenditure
of the State, and one-seventh is tithe.

(3) The sterile class consists of craftsmen, artisans,
manufacturers, shopkeepers, merchants, traffickers.
This class is the appendage to the two former classes.
It is at its best a *classe stipendiée*, a salaried class, and
on the whole a *classe subordonnée*. In the physiocratic
realm the towns are subordinate to the countryside,
quite as much as in medieval society to the barons and
abbots. The "citadins" depend for their livelihood on
the expenditure of the Court, the nobility, the prelates
and the gentry.

The mass of money (*pécule nationale*) consists of
three milliards, two of which are in the possession of
the producers, the third in that of the sterile class. The
money is not regarded as an indispensable or integral
part of the national economy: it is not real wealth, but
a medium of exchange; its only function is to facilitate
the circulation of the consumable goods which man

needs for his self-preservation. For, in the absence of money, the distribution of the produce would none the less go on, though cumbrously. On the other hand, in the absence of real wealth no amount of money could secure to man his self-preservation.

The prosperity of agriculture, and therefore of the realm, will be promoted if the following conditions are adhered to: (i) Freedom of tillage; no restrictions on the mode of cultivation, that is, abolition of the traditional restrictions which bound the cultivators to primitive and medieval rules and customs, so that it can be carried on on large-scale holdings with the most appropriate instruments. Freedom from all sorts of impositions, that is, abolition of *taille, aides, dues,* etc. (ii) The price *pro setier* (twelve bushels) gravitates round eighteen livres. This is the *bon prix*, the just price, which will be arrived at by the free play of supply and demand, for such a price covers cost of labour, farmers' sustenance, and the value added by the fertility of the soil. (iii) Unobstructed and uninterrupted circulation of the goods, agricultural as well as manufactured, throughout the realm. (iv) Equal freedom for foreign trade, inconsiderable as it may be, for this will reduce the *faux-frais* and will also lessen the opportunity of the merchants and traffickers to obtain the surplus of goods at low prices or to sell the imported commodities at high prices, "car la police du commerce intérieur et extérieur la plus sure, la plus exacte, la plus profitable à la nation et à l'État consiste dans la plaine liberté de la concurrence" (p. 336).

(b) *Production, Distribution, and Circulation*.—We are now approaching the *Tableau* itself, on which so many keen minds exercised their wits at the time of its publication and many years later. In order to appreciate its difficulties we shall first give Quesnay's own exposition and his diagram of it (pp. 310–314).

"*Producers*	"*Proprietors*	"*Sterile Class*
The *avances annuelles* amount to two milliards. They produce goods to the value of five milliards, of which two milliards are *produit net* or revenue for the proprietors."	Revenue or *produit net*: two milliards. They buy for one milliard victuals from the producers, and for the other milliard they buy commodities and merchandise from the sterile class."	"*Avances annuelles*: one milliard, for which they buy raw materials from the producers."[1]

Quesnay continues to explain:

Thus the producers sell produce for one milliard money to the proprietors; and they sell also raw materials to the sterile class for one milliard money.

The producers possess now   ..   ..   2 milliards

The proprietors buy for their second milliard various commodities and merchandise from the sterile class, which, in its turn, buys with this milliard victuals (sustenance) for its members from the producers.

The producers thus receive one milliard more   ..   ..   ..   1 milliard

The total sum of purchases by the proprietors and by the sterile class from the producers amounts to..   ..   ..   ..   3 milliards

---

[1] According to Abbé Baudeau, the commentator and friend of Quesnay, the sterile class has no share in the *pécule nationale*, but starts its annual production with one milliard commodities (from

Of those three milliards received by the producers two milliards are paid by them as revenue or *produit net* to the proprietors for the current year, and the third milliard is spent by the producers on the purchase of manufactured commodities and merchandise from the sterile class. This milliard is retained by the sterile class to replace the milliard circulating capital, which was spent on raw materials. Thus we see that the sterile class does not increase its capital in the process of its work.

Quesnay, continuing his explanatory remarks on the non-productive work of the craftsmen and manufacturers, supports his view by the following argument.

The raw materials and the labour of the sterile class give the commodities the value of two milliards, one of which is spent on the purchase of sustenance for the agents who compose that class. We see that there is only consumption and annihilation of production, but no (increased) reproduction; this class subsists only on the successive payments as retribution of its labour, for which it obtains sustenance. The milliard money which it retains will be employed in the ensuing year on the purchase of raw materials.

We have seen that the three milliards, which the

the last year), which it sells to the proprietors (E. Daire, *Les Physiocrats*, "Explication du Tableau Économique," p. 863). This would mean that the craftsmen originally obtained raw materials from the productive class for work performed in the villages in the production of some parts of the fixed capital (buildings, vehicles, ploughs, etc.).

producers receive from the sale of produce (to the proprietors one milliard and from the sales of produce
and raw materials to the sterile class two milliards),
are used by the producers for the payment of revenue
(*produit net*) to the proprietors, and for the purchase
of commodities and merchandise from the sterile
class for one milliard. This accounts only for three
milliards reproduction. We know, however, that the
whole annual reproduction was five milliards, so that
we have still to account for two milliards produce.
Now, these two milliards produce replace the circulating capital (*avances annuelles*), which amounts to
two milliards, and serves as such for the ensuing year.
There thus remain in the hands of the producers two
milliards produce and one milliard commodities and
merchandise. This total of three milliards forms the
reprises, the returns of agriculture. Of this total the
producers use two milliards produce as circulating
capital for the ensuing year's cultivation, and one
milliard represents the *intérêts* of 10 per cent on the
fixed capital of ten milliards; this one milliard "interest" is used for repair of the wear and tear of the
fixed capital, and as reserves for emergencies, such as
blight, hail, floods, fire, loss of live-stock through
disease and death.

Quesnay gives the following *resumé*:

"Le total de 5 milliards, partagé d'abord entre la
classe productive et la classe des propriétaires, étant
dépensé annuellement dans un ordre régulier qui
assure perpétuellement la même reproduction annuelle,

il y a un milliard qui est dépensé par les propriétaires en achats faits à la classe productive et un milliard en achats à la classe stérile. La classe productive qui vend pour 3 milliards de production aux deux autres classes, en rend 2 milliards pour le payment du revenue aux propriétaires et en dépense 1 milliard en achats qu'elle fait à la classe stérile: ainsi la classe stérile reçoit deux milliards qu'elle emploie à la classe productive en achats pour la subsistance de ses agents et pour les matières premières de ses ouvrages; et la classe productive dépense elle-même annuellement pour deux milliards de productions, ce qui complette la dépense ou la consomnation totale de cinq milliards de reproduction annuelle" (p. 313).

(c) *The* Formule du Tableau (*diagram*).

We have paraphrased and reproduced (p. 155–158) the essential passages of Quesnay's commentary on his *Tableau*. On page 159 we reproduce the *Formule du Tableau* or the diagram illustrating the circulation of the produce.

This *Formule* is not particularly enlightening. The three oblique dotted lines running parallel from left to right (or from right to left) and the two oblique intersecting dotted lines running from the top downwards, indicate the purchases and sales between the three classes.

The proprietors buy victuals for one milliard from the producers, and for the other milliard they buy commodities and merchandise from the sterile class.

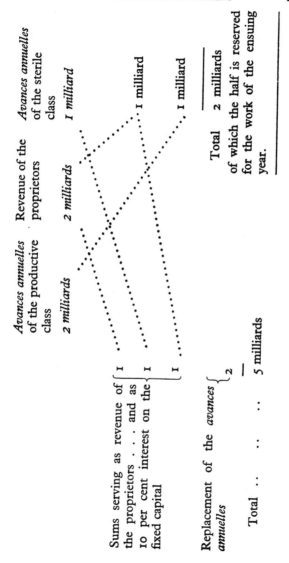

Avances annuelles of the productive class	Revenue of the proprietors	*Avances annuelles* of the sterile class
2 milliards	*2 milliards*	*1 milliard*

Sums serving as revenue of the proprietors . . . and as 10 per cent interest on the fixed capital

$$\left.\begin{array}{c} 1 \\ 1 \\ 1 \end{array}\right\}$$

Replacement of the *avances annuelles* $\Big\}$ 2

Total .. .. .. 5 milliards

1 milliard

1 milliard

Total 2 milliards
of which the half is reserved
for the work of the ensuing
year.

The sterile class buys from the producers raw materials for its milliard money (circulating capital), fashions them into commodities, sells them to the proprietors and the producers for the total of two milliards. The labour of the sterile class added to the raw materials, as it would seem, a value of one milliard, but it does not represent a new or an increased value: this milliard is merely the value of the sustenance which the sterile class consumed in the course of the manufacturing process. The sterile class spent or "annihilated" goods for two milliards (raw materials for one milliard, and victuals for another milliard), and received in return two milliards.

The producers, starting with two milliards *avances annuelles* (agricultural produce and commodities), produce goods for the value of five milliards. They sell for one milliard produce to the proprietors, for another milliard produce to the sterile class, and for another milliard raw materials also to the sterile class. Total: three milliard proceeds. They pay two milliards as revenue (*produit net*) to the proprietors, and buy commodities and merchandise from the sterile class for one milliard. Of the original five milliards goods, which they had produced in their annual cultivation, three milliards are thus assounted for. There remains still in their hands two milliards produce. If we now add the one milliard commodities and merchandise (which the producers bought from the sterile class) to the two milliards produce, the producers emerged from their annual cultivation with three milliards goods: two are used for the ensuing year's cultivation, and one milliard as *intérêts* (repair of wear and tear, reserves for emergencies).

Such are the elucidations obtained from Quesnay's observations on the *Tableau*. They raise, however, several questions, which are still waiting for an answer: Where do the proprietors get the means to purchase produce and commodities? We might assume from the *Tableau* that the producers did only pay the two milliards *produit net* after having sold produce to the proprietors and to the sterile class, so that the proprietors had bought goods before they obtained the wherewithal to pay for them. Further, the sterile class buys according to the *Tableau* for its circulating capital of one milliard raw materials from the producers, makes commodities, and sells them to the proprietors. The question is, how could the artisans, etc., do their work without having victuals to live upon? The *Tableau* fails likewise to show the fixed capital (workshops, tools, trading stalls) of the sterile class. Finally, the *Tableau* allows to the proprietors and the producers commodities and merchandise for one milliard each, but none, absolutely none, to the sterile class, as if the artisans, shopkeepers, merchants, needed no lodgings, clothing, utensils, and some comforts!

3. *Elucidation of the* Tableau

We can find logically satisfactory answers to those puzzling questions only if we strictly adhere to the principles and observations of Quesnay, and if we regard the data of his *Tableau* as ultimate results of his analysis, thus allowing us some latitude for rearranging the various operations or the details of the distribution and circulation.

The economic year starts with the bringing in of the harvest (corn, vegetables, increase of live-stock, wool, flax, timber, wine). This would be about October of any year. In order to simplify the dates we identify the economic year with the calendar year, say, January 1940. At the beginning of 1940, then, the producers start with their portion of the *pécule nationale*, that is, with two milliards money and the harvest, the total reproduction of real wealth in 1939, which is estimated at five milliards.

Those five milliards reproduction were obtained from a two milliards outlay in kind (*avances annuelles*) made in 1939—a gross increase of three milliards. The net increase (*produit net*) is two milliards, for, as we know, one milliard is reckoned by the producers to meet the *intérêts*, that is, cost of repair of the wear and tears of the fixed capital, and repair of the contingent damage by blight, hail, fire, floods, disease, and death of live-stock.

The proprietors, as stated previously, have no share in the national mass of money (*pécule nationale*); they can only obtain money from the productive class. They need money for their own expenditure and for the single tax, that is, for public revenue and tithe. The productive class remits now to them the *produit net* in two milliards money. It is only at this point that the circulation can make a start.

The effective demand for goods, for real wealth, makes itself soon felt. The proprietors buy victuals for one milliard from the producers; the sterile class, expecting orders from the proprietors, likewise buys for its milliard (circulating capital) raw materials and victuals from the producers, and fashions commodities for one milliard. These commodities are purchased by the proprietors for their second milliard of the *produit net*. At the end of 1940 the proprietors had spent their two milliards.

The sterile class received its milliard (circulating capital) back consequent upon their sales to the proprietors.

The producers have likewise received their two milliards money back: one milliard for the produce they sold to the proprietors, and the other milliard for the raw materials and produce which they sold to the sterile class; but their stock (that is, the yield of their harvest) was reduced by two-fifths, and they are in need of commodities and merchandise. The sterile class is aware of that demand, and it buys for its milliard again raw materials and produce and fashions commodities, which are bought by the producers for that milliard that they had received for their produce and raw materials from the sterile class.

At the end of 1940 the position of the sterile class and the producers is now this: The sterile class made or procured commodities and merchandise for two milliards, but consumed victuals for one milliard, so that they are left with one milliard money to be used for the work of the ensuing year 1941. Its operations produced no increase of wealth. The producers sold three-fifths of their harvest: two milliards victuals (one to the proprietors, the other to the sterile class), and also for one milliard raw materials to the sterile class, but bought commodities and merchandise from the latter for one milliard, which they retain. At the end of 1940 the producers have still at their disposal for two milliards produce, which they will use for cultivation in 1940 and thus replace their circulating capital in kind, which they had used up in 1939 for the harvest at their disposal in 1940; and they have also for one milliard manufactured commodities and merchandise, the value of which serves as *intérêts*, that is, for repair of the wear and tear of the fixed capital and the contingent losses through blight, floods, fire, etc.

The physiocratic realm, as its economy demonstrates, is a realm of a medieval type. It is intended by its author to preserve in perpetuity its stable equilibrium. The peasantry and the craftsmen are steadily working for their own sustenance; and the net surplus is surrendered to the small number of the lords of the land who administer the State. The share of the proprietors or governing class (two milliards) is as large as the share of the producers (two milliards) though the latter share includes also the expense on cultivation, and though the number of the producers is one-half of the whole population, while the number of the governing class is less than a quarter of the population.

For all the elucidation of the *Tableau*, we are still in the dark on two points. We learned that the proprietors and the producers are provided with commodities and merchandise, but no provision in that respect is made for the sterile class. This is one obscure point. The other point concerns the absence of fixed capital in the hands of the sterile class. Where does this class work or sell its commodities?

The question concerning the first point appears to have engaged the attention of contemporary friends of Quesnay. Abbé Nicolas Baudeau, the editor of the *Ephémérides du Citoyen*, a monthly publication, to which Quesnay contributed, wrote in his paper, in form of letters to a lady, a long commentary (*Explication*) on the *Tableau* (reprinted in Daire's *Les Physiocrates*, pp. 823–867). On account of its epistolary form, the *Explication* is sometimes unbearably elementary and diffuse; but it contains some good suggestions, which, considering Baudeau's close connection with Quesnay, may be regarded as authoritative (*ibid.*, pp. 854, 863). Without entering into the details, on which Baudeau expatiates, it is sufficient for our purpose to accept his idea that the sterile class raised the price of its commodities and merchandise, and from the profit thus made provided itself with the necessary commodities and comforts.

Let us now see how the craftsmen and traders obtain their commodities and merchandise. We learned from

the *Tableau* that the proprietors and the producers buy
from the sterile class for one milliard each. The sterile
class, however, does not give value for value, that is,
not one milliard's worth of commodities, but only two-
thirds of a milliard. It raises the price by $33\frac{1}{3}$ per cent.
The proprietors and producers receive for their two
milliards from the sterile class commodities to the value
of only $666\frac{1}{3} \cdot 2 = 1,332\frac{2}{3}$ million livres, so that the
sterile class obtains an amount of commodities and
merchandise equal to that of each of the two other
classes.

Abbé Baudeau's solution of the problem is quite in
conformity with Quesnay's economic doctrine that the
tradespeople raise the price of the goods, and that the
charge falls ultimately on the productive class.

The question as to the omission of all reference in
the *Tableau* to the fixed capital of the sterile class
remains, so far, unanswered. The craftsmen and the
tradespeople in general must have had shops and tools
for their work; stalls and counters for their sales. I
cannot give any positive answer to this question, but
I venture to put forward an idea which may be worth
taking into consideration, and which is quite in agreement with my general view that Quesnay was thinking
in medieval terms.

In the early Middle Ages many artisans and craftsmen worked on the manors. Here they had their
smithies for fashioning swords and coats of mail; rooms
for the tailors and bootmakers, shops for the carpenters had existed on great estates; and it may be—

students may inquire into this—that in the market towns the stalls of the merchants were also seignorial properties.

In a former chapter it was pointed out that Quesnay regarded the unproductive class as an appendage to the proprietors and producers, and he may have had in his mind that these two classes will provide the *class subordonnée* with suitably furnished places to work in and to carry on its trades.

4. *The Neo-Medieval Society*

Quesnay's main endeavour in the last two decades of his life was to re-create a medieval society which should be of greater permanency and excellence than the old one had been. At the head of his ideal society we see a single ruler, a pious king, who subjects himself to the law of nature. There are in his realm no legislators, nor man-made laws, but a council of jurists interpreting the tenets of *ius naturale*, quite in the same manner as the Spiritual Lords and Canon lawyers in the Middle Ages interpreted, for the benefit of the Christian king, the laws of God.

There are in this ideal realm three estates, similar to those of the old feudal society: (i) The nobility and the clergy, who own the lands and bear the whole burden of administration, defence, and spiritual care. This burden is represented by the single tax of the landowners, from which the State expenditure is met. (ii) The cultivators of the land—the *villeins* in the

Middle Ages—carry on the agriculture, create the *produit net*, which is paid as tribute to the nobility, while the cultivators, the real producers, receive no other reward than sustenance. (iii) The tradespeople and merchants, the unproductive class, the members of which—like the gilds of the Middle Ages—transform the raw materials into commodities, the value of which amounts to that of their labour and expenses; or they supply goods to the consumers, and gain—by raising the price—a moderate gain as a wage or salary as reward of their services. The gilds depended for the sales of their commodities on the nobility, the clergy, and peasantry. In the neo-medieval society this class depends on the expenditure made by the proprietors of the land and the cultivators. The method of exchange is, however, different, for unlike the members of the craft gilds who buy their victuals at statutory prices, the unproductive class of the ideal society buys its raw materials and victuals in free competition either direct from the cultivators or through the intermediary of the local tradesmen. Quesnay, based on the law of nature, regarded natural liberty as a better safeguard of the just price than statutory fixing of prices.

The trafficker, the *marchand revendeur*, is a merchant-alien. He has no home in the realm. He is a member of the universal mercantile republic—as in the Middle Ages the Genoese, the Lombard, the Jew, the Easterling, the Syrian, accumulating pecuniary riches by *triche*, by enhancing the prices of commodities, that is, depriving the productive class of large parts of its produce. He is doing business anywhere, and will do anything. The alien merchants are also the money-lenders, and must be subjected to usury laws. The number of merchants and traffickers is kept at its absolutely necessary minimum, so that there is least opportunity for diminishing the national fund of riches and for corrupting the morals of the citizens. It is all as written by Aquinas and Fénelon.

Money plays a minor part in medieval society; it is a medium of exchange in foreign trade and local markets. It is brought into the country mainly for the king's exchequer. In the neo-medieval society, the pecuniary riches are a fixed store of counters; they are not regarded as real wealth, since its quantity and its pledging power depend on the magnitude of the real wealth produced annually by the cultivators.

We are in the presence of a static society, as medieval society was, prior to the rise of the mercantilist balance of trade and the spread of manufacture. Its wealth is limited by the annual yield of agriculture and is distributed according to the status of the three estates. There is no dynamic class pressing on its limits, or disturbing the stable equilibrium: there is no urge for expansion. The growth of the population is dependent on the annual produce. There are no inventions. The craftsmen are working in the workshops, either their own or provided by the nobility and abbots. They are fashioning the things which the proprietors, the clergy, and the other inhabitants need for house and homestead in weekdays or during festivals. There is no laying up of pecuniary riches or treasure; the inhabitants are spending their incomes as they receive them. The gifts of the earth, secured by tillage, and the un-obstructed flow of real wealth through the body politic, secure to all its members their necessaries according to their status in society.

The ideal realm is a rationalized medieval society which deals out distributive justice to the various orders; some receiving more from the national fund, some less, all according to the social status of each: *suum cuique*. This realm, through its economic liberty, allows commutative justice, equality of exchanges to be the rule between vendor and buyer. Moreover, by removing the traditional restrictions on tillage, agri-cultural produce is considerably increased, and the classes enjoy larger shares of the national fund. It is a neo-medieval society, which negates mercantilism, rejects the balance of trade policy, and corrects some of the shortcomings of old medieval society, which knew no liberty for the villein in his tillage, nor free play of supply and demand to determine the *iustum pretium*, the just and good price between buyer and seller.

IX

THE PHYSIOCRATIC SCHOOL

1. *Adam Smith's Opinion*

The year of the publication of the *Wealth of Nations* was the last of the twenty years (1756–1776) in which physiocracy flourished, attracting the attention and gaining the adherence of political writers, jurists, and theologians. When Quesnay died (1774) the fame of his economic teaching was nearing its culminating point. In that year the intendant of Limoges, A. R. J. Turgot, was raised to the office of Finance Minister. Though he cannot be regarded as an orthodox physiocrat—he abhorred the term and essence of *despotisme légal*, and he was against usury laws—he went a long way with the adherents of Quesnay; and on entering his high office he appointed one of the best-known physiocrats, Dupont de Nemours, as his assistant. Turgot's work as finance minister was of comparatively short duration. His zeal in introducing in rapid succession a series of liberal reforms proved his undoing. In 1776 he was dismissed. His retirement marks the beginning of the decline of physiocracy, though it still counted for some years several writers and public men among its adherents in France, England, Germany, and Russia.

Adam Smith had the highest opinion of Quesnay,

to whom he refers as "the very ingenious and profound author" of the "*œconomic table*." Had Quesnay's life been prolonged for a few years, Smith, it is said, would have dedicated his great work to him. An instructive chapter of the *Wealth of Nations* (book iv, chap. 9) is given to a review of the strength and weakness of physiocracy. As pointed out before, Smith rejects the view of the physiocratic school that manufacture is sterile: that it is but reproducing the values of the raw materials and the cost of labour without increasing them, but "with all the imperfections of this system, it is, perhaps, the nearest approximation to the truth that has yet been published upon the subject of political economy, and is upon that account well worth the consideration of every man who wishes to examine with attention the principles of that very important science." The notion that labour employed on the land was alone productive might be regarded as too narrow; "yet, in representing the wealth of nations as consisting, not in the unconsumable riches of money, but in the consumable goods annually reproduced by the labour of society," furthermore, "in representing perfect liberty as the only effectual expedient for rendering this annual reproduction the greatest possible, its doctrine seems to be in every respect as just as it is generous and liberal."

It is, as we see, the anti-mercantilism of Quesnay which aroused Smith's admiration for him: the repudiation of money as the essence of wealth, and the condemnation of authoritative interference with economic activities. Moreover, Smith was in agreement with Quesnay not only with regard to the reproduction of real wealth and the beneficial effect of perfect liberty, but also with regard to rent—namely, that the rent of land, or what Quesnay called the *produit net*—owed its existence to the fertility of the soil. "The rent," declares Smith, "may be considered as the produce of those powers of Nature, the use of which the landlord lends to the farmer. . . . It is the work of Nature which remains after deducting or compensating everything which can be regarded as the work of man. It is seldom less than a fourth, and frequently more than a third of the whole produce (book iv, chap. 5). Quesnay put the contribution of nature or the *produit net* at two-fifths, but the principle is the same.

2. *Quesnay, Smith, and Ricardo on Rent*

This short chapter, though a digression, is still pertinent to our treatment of physiocracy as it affected British economics. It may also contribute to a better apprehension of Ricardo's conception of rent.

From the latter half of the seventeenth century, when economists began to think of the nature of rent, to about the middle of the eighteenth century, or roughly from Petty to Hume, it was assumed that rent on land was something like interest on money. The owner of land and the owner of money let or lent their respective instruments of production and commerce to farmers and merchants, who then surrendered a part of their profits or gains to the landlord and money-lord. The payment to the former was called rent, the payment to the other was called interest. The rate of each depended on supply and demand.

With the advance of the eighteenth century, when rents were rising, the opinion gained adherence that the land produced "three rents: one went to the landlord, the other third for the charges of cultivation, the remaining third for the support of the farmer and his family."[1] Another writer of the period (Richard Cantillon) likewise declared: "Farmers earn three rents."[2] The concept of rent, as may be inferred from those statements, was not clearly defined; sometimes it meant the whole produce of the land, sometimes only the net produce or profit, and sometimes exclusively that part of the net produce which was paid to the landlord. Petty, for instance, uses the term rent in two senses: net produce (profit) and payment to the landlord: in the latter sense he uses the phrase "rent on land."[3] But, however undefined the term "rent" was, the opinion in the eighteenth century was general that its existence was mainly due to the inherent powers of the soil.

Boisguillebert and Cantillon set great store by the soil as source of wealth; Quesnay looked upon it as the only source of riches. Smith, likewise, following the trend of thought common in the eighteenth century,

[1] *An apology for the business of pawn-broking*, 1744 (reprinted in McCulloch's *Miscellaneous Economical Tracts*, 1857, p. 154).

[2] R. Cantillon, *Essai sur la nature du commerce*, ed. 1931, pp. 43, 123.   [3] See the author's *Early British Economists*, p. 171.

declared that capital employed on land yielded not only the average profit on stock, but a rent for the landlord. It was a sort of extra profit, and it was due to the operation of the natural powers of the soil, whereas in manufacture that co-operation on the part of nature was missing. That was the reason why capital employed in manufacture was less profitable than in agriculture, and brought only the ordinary rate of profit.[1]

Ricardo was dissatisfied with the current theories of "rent," and the undefined, loose meaning given to it. Is rent something like interest on money—a part of the farmer's gains on the hired land? Or is it an extra-profit, which is not obtained in any other trade?

Smith answers affirmatively—rent is an extra-profit and it arises from the natural powers of the soil. This reply is not acceptable to Ricardo, for, if Smith's statement had any basis in fact, then there would rule in the market simultaneously and permanently two rates of profit. Now the actual state of the market shows that that is economically absurd. But this *reductio ad absurdum* by no means invalidates the statement that

[1] A. Smith writes: "No equal capital puts into motion a greater quantity of productive labour than that of the farmer. Not only his labouring servants, but his labouring cattle, are productive labourers. In Agriculture, too, Nature labours along with man. . . . And its produce has its value, as well as that of the most expensive workmen. . . . No equal quantity of productive labour employed in manufacture can ever occasion so great reproduction. . . . The capital employed in agriculture adds a much greater value to the annual produce of the land and labour of the country, to the real wealth and revenue of the inhabitants" (*Wealth of Nations*, book ii, chap. 5, ed. Cannan, vol. i, p. 343. This is nearly all Quesnay, even the terminology).

rent is paid or obtained from an extra-profit. Ricardo denies only that it is a gift of nature or that it is something permanent. According to him, it is due to the growth of trade, commerce, and population, which raise the demand for foodstuffs and raw materials. And, as the corn laws prevent the import of foreign supplies, the growing demand leads to inferior classes of land being taken into cultivation. Now, inferior lands require more labour, and since labour is the measure of value, and marginal labour[1] regulates the price of all commodities, it follows necessarily that the relatively better classes of land, though requiring less labour, reap the higher prices which arise from employing marginal labour, or from employing capital on marginal lands.

Rent, according to Ricardo, is only that part of the farmer's payment which does not come from the ordinary rate of profit on his capital, but from the higher price of the produce. Not all payments of the farmer to the landlord deserve the appellation "rent." A farmer has always to pay the hire of the land, but rent does not begin before inferior lands are taken into cultivation: only in those circumstances does an extra-profit arise on the relatively better classes of land.

[1] Marginal labour is defined by Ricardo as follows: "The exchangeable value of all commodities, whether they be manufactured, or the produce of the land, is always regulated, not by the less quantity of labour that will suffice for their production under circumstances highly favourable . . . but by the greater quantity of labour necessarily bestowed on their production . . . under the most unfavourable circumstances" (*Principles of Political Economy and Taxation*, third edition, p. 37).

This extra-profit forms the major part of rent. It is paid in addition to the ordinary hire of the land. And it is the effect of the growth of trade, commerce, and population, as well as of the corn laws.

Ricardo stood in need of a De Quincey to make his theory of rent intelligible. Had there arisen such an interpreter, he would have explained that according to the master there is absolute rent and differential rent. The former corresponds to the normal rate of profit; the latter is the extra-profit. And it is the differential rent which enriches the landlord, and which arises from the effects of the growth of trade, commerce, and population. This formulation of Ricardo's theory of rent appears to be capable of removing the difficulties which are assumed to be in the way of accepting it as valid.

Ricardo's theory of rent is uncompromisingly opposed to physiocracy. It tells the nobility and the landed interests in general that the so-called "sterile class," or the class employed in trade and commerce, far from being unproductive and utterly dependent on the patronage of the nobility, is in reality the source of rent, that is, of the great part of the revenue on which the nobility lived. Ricardo's economics does more; it tells the mercantilists that riches do not arise in trafficking, since foreign trade, if allowed full freedom, is an exchange of commodities, different in quality and shape, but equal in their labour quantities. Riches arise from capital and labour employed in factories, mines, and fields, and their value is augmented by the merchants bringing the goods to the consumers. Finally, Ricardo refutes Smith's view that capital employed in agriculture is *per se* more profitable than that employed in manufacture.

To sum up: Quesnay, morally and emotionally in opposition to the economic policy of his time and country, became neo-medieval. Adam Smith witnessed the inception of the factory system and machine age in agricultural surroundings; his economics reflects both. Ricardo saw the industrial revolution in its full development; he was the economist of the industrial and mercantile middle class, which was aspiring to political power and which regarded itself as the backbone of the nation.

3. *The Physiocratic Sect*

Adam Smith was not particularly impressed by the doctrinal contributions of the physiocratic writers who surrounded or followed their master. They formed a sect, and wrote numerous books on their doctrines, dealing not only with political economy proper, but with every aspect of civil government. There was hardly any originality or variety in their works; they all followed implicitly the teaching of Quesnay. Their admiration for him, "a man of the greatest modesty and simplicity," knew no bounds. The Marquis de Mirabeau went so far as to pronounce the *Tableau Économique* to be one of the three supreme inventions of mankind, the other two having been the invention of writing and the invention of money. Moreover, the *Tableau Économique* completed the other two (*Wealth of Nations*, book iv, chap. 9).

Adam Smith's high appreciation of Quesnay as an original economist, and the much less favourable opinion he held of the followers, are worthy of notice. He was displeased with their lack of any critical attitude towards the master. He called them disparagingly a sect.

What is a sect—and what is a school of thought?

A sect consists of a number of votaries, who regard themselves as the only legitimate custodians of the body of doctrines which the master transmitted to them. They think it their main duty to stand up in its defence from violation.

A school of thought or an intellectual movement, while respecting the master's legacy and not easily induced to question any of its doctrines on the promptings of an opponent, yet inquires into them, removes the untenable, and preserves what is adaptable to the progress of time.

Once a sect is formed, the members regard it as their duty and as a *point d'honneur* to prove as valid every doctrine which goes to compose the system. They do not necessarily agree with every particular of it, but they are all united in the conviction that the master is of superior intelligence, and that the foundation of the system is well laid. This is the common measure, the bond which keeps the sect together, all else is accepted either from logical operation or from faith, where reason proves insufficient to demonstrate the truth of any of the doctrines. There is, besides, the human weakness which makes us ashamed, particularly in the presence of opponents, to admit that we are not equal to the intellectual effort of comprehending and defending what the master promulgated and transmitted.

Those who were once members, as the writer was, of the old Marxist sect will all the better understand the physiocratic sect, and the gravamen of Smith's accusation levelled at the followers of Quesnay. He was greatly displeased with the physiocratic followers professing to understand the doctrine of the sterility of manufacture, which no ordinary man was able to grasp, still less to defend.

Dupont de Nemours took notice of Smith's critical view of the physiocratic school, and in his eulogy on Turgot (1782) referred also to the *Wealth of Nations*:

"What there is of true teaching in this estimable work, but troublesome (*pénible*) to read in two thick volumes, is to be found in Turgot's *Réflexions sur la formation et la distribution des richesses*. And what Adam Smith added lacks precision and even a basis." This is a sweeping statement. Dupont—according to his biographer—gradually came to see the injustice of it, and he excused his former opinion by reference to his deficient knowledge of English at the time.[1]

[1] G. Schelle, *Dupont de Nemours*, Paris, 1888, p. 159

4. *Of Quesnay's Followers*

The members of the school were united in the philosophy of the law of nature, in the thought of the necessity of freedom of trade, and in the endeavour to promote the interests of agriculture. This was the doctrinal essence, the common measure of the various personal factors comprising the School. All were distinguished by a cosmopolitan outlook, love of humanity, and an ardent desire for the establishment of peaceful intercourse between nations. The motto of Dupont de Nemours, "Liberté, Ordre, Progrès," would have been acceptable to all of them. They were good liberals, genuine types of the humanitarianism of the second half of the eighteenth century—one of the noblest periods in the history of secular thought and ethics. They gathered round the master because of his economic philosophy, which appeared to them the clearest and most sober voice of those thoughts and desires.

As to the other doctrines of the master, they were, as a rule, accepted from faith and supported by reasoning within the limits of faith. Hence it came about that the commentaries, written by the leading adherents of the School on the doctrines of Quesnay, offered, as Smith complained, so little variety or independent judgment. On what they regarded as the main doctrines there was no difference of opinion.

Differences of opinion, and the necessity for independent inquiries, could have made themselves felt only if Quesnay had attempted to build up a neo-medieval or neo-feudal realm. Only at such a point would his followers have become conscious that the master meant something more or much less than liberalism, at any rate, something different. As long as the *Tableau* remained a piece of paper with zigzag lines—or the *zizacs*, as the *Tableau* was known among the ladies and gentlemen of the Versailles Court—all was harmony in the School.

Writing these pages on Physiocracy, the thought of its similarity with the Marxist School has often suggested itself to my mind. As long as Marxism remained a philosophical or sociological set of doctrines, all socialists were united. The common measure of all of us was: (i) social reform in favour of the working class, and (ii) democracy. All Marxists were Social Democrats, and we all interpreted Marxism in the same terms. There was hardly any serious variety or independent judgment. All was harmony in the School. When, however, a crisis came, and some action in conformity with our views had to be taken, differences of opinion came to the surface, and we learned that Marx meant incessant, intense class war, bankruptcy of capitalism, dictatorship of the proletariat, forcible dispossession of the bourgeoisie. And then there was an end of the old harmony: we had revisionists, syndicalists, revolutionary socialists, Mensheviks, Bolsheviks, and books galore on Marxism.

Physiocracy never reached the stage of action or crisis, and therefore no real analysis was undertaken, and no development or differentiation of its doctrines took place. I believe that the views expressed in these pages on Quesnay's economics are the first attempt at a re-examination and an understanding of its meaning and its implications.

Well, there was no necessity for Quesnay's followers to do more than to popularize the teaching of their master, and they all performed their work in an excellent manner.

The premier disciple and missionary of Quesnay was Victor Riquetti Marquis de Mirabeau (1715–1789), known also as the elder Mirabeau, whose son was the great orator in the first years of the French Revolution. He participated in all progressive movements of his time, read a good many English works, and published in 1756 his first economic book, entitled *L'Ami des Hommes*, with the sub-title *Traité de la Population*. Quesnay read the book, and found it in its main thesis to be on a wrong track, but in many subordinate points on the way to truth. He made the acquaintance of the author, and told him that in making the population the source of wealth he was setting the plough before the oxen; and that the writers upon whom he had drawn, notably Cantillon, the author of the *Essai sur la nature du commerce*, were a set of fools.[1] Quesnay gradually won him over to the views later called physiocracy. When he published his *Tableau Économique*, Mirabeau became his disciple and popularizer, as was mentioned in a former chapter. Adam Smith calls him a "diligent and respectable author."

[1] Loménie, *Les Mirabeau*, vol. ii, p. 172.

It was, however, not Mirabeau, but Le Mercier de la Rivière (1719–1792), who popularized Quesnay's economics for the large public in France and abroad. His *L'Ordre naturel et essentiel des sociétés politiques* (1767) was in every way a success. It was published in London in a quarto of five hundred pages and in Paris in two volumes, 12°, and its sale was rapid and relatively large—three thousand copies. Adam Smith writes of it: "The most distinct and best connected account of the doctrine is to be found in a little book written by Mr. Mercier de la Rivière, entitled *The natural and essential order of political societies*." The adjective "little" is puzzling. Either Smith confused the size of Le Mercier's book with that of some other book, or he used the adjective "little" not in a quantitative but in a qualitative sense, as compared with the greatness of Quesnay's work. Le Mercier's commentary is with regard to style and closely reasoned argumentation a veritable masterpiece, though of the forty-four chapters which it contains no more than the last ten (xxxiv–xliv) may be said to be of direct relevance to Quesnay's economic doctrines. The author devoted too many chapters to problems of *despotisme légal* and taxation, but he excels in persuasive advocacy for all those points where Quesnay's economics offer difficulties to modern common sense.

It is evident from his book that its author was of the legal profession, and a public officer of great experience in State finance. He became an intimate friend and disciple of Quesnay in 1759, and soon after he was appointed intendant of Martinique; but in his methods of colonial administration he attempted to translate his free trade doctrine into practice and met with the hostility of the metropolitan mercantile interests, which finally enforced his dismissal. His crime consisted in facilitating commercial intercourse between the French colonies and the New England traders.

After the publication of the *L'Ordre naturel*, which spread the fame of its author far and wide, influential personages of the St. Petersburg Court induced the Empress Catherine II to invite him in order to compose a code of laws for Russia. Le Mercier came, saw, but did not conquer. The adjective *légal*, qualifying the *despotisme*, was evidently no recommendation. He returned to Paris, where he was active as a writer to the end of his life.

Pierre S. Dupont de Nemours (1739–1817) was the journalist, editor, and secretary of the physiocratic school. Everything that came from the pen of Quesnay or Le Mercier was "sublime." He edited the *Journal de l'Agriculture, du Commerce et des Finance*, the organ of free discussion supplementing the *Gazette du Commerce*, from 1765 to 1766, and the *Ephémérides du Citoyen* (a periodical established by Baudeau in 1765) from the year 1768 onwards.

In 1767 Quesnay handed to him for purpose of publication a collection of his essays, dialogues, etc. Dupont issued them under the famous title *La Physiocratie*, introducing it with a long *Discours* of his own, but one of the articles given to him by Quesnay was not included. It was an article which argued for the authoritative fixing of the rate of interest. With all his reverence and admiration for his master, he, the good liberal he was, could not stomach government interference in trade matters.

Dupont, as mentioned before, served as Turgot's assistant in the Finance Ministry, 1774–1776. This association with Turgot gave him in later years a high standing in political circles and brought him into contact with foreign diplomats, notably with Benjamin Franklin. He was instrumental in the drafting of the commercial treaty between France and England in 1786. Four years later he was elected to the Constituent Assembly, and spoke there against the issue of assignates. Quesnay's doctrine concerning real wealth and pecuniary riches stood him in good stead in his argument that paper money was no remedy against a financial crisis.

Later on he emigrated to America, and finally settled in New Jersey. As the friend of Turgot and Franklin, he was also befriended by Jefferson. His descendants are now the American millionaires and munition makers of the same name.

Much more scholarly, but with less *savoir-faire* than Dupont, was Abbé Nicolas Baudeau (1730–1792). He studied theology, and was appointed professor, but abandoned his professorship, and turned to journalism. He established the periodical *Ephémérides du Citoyen* in 1765, and opposed physiocracy, but was converted in 1766 by Le Trosne. We have given above Bauedau's contribution to the elucidation of the *Tableau Économique*.

G. F. Le Trosne (1728–1780) was a jurist and scholar, and practised at Orleans. He was one of the earliest converts to Quesnay's teaching. He likewise wrote a popularization of it, entitled *L'Intérêt Social* He was the only member of the physiocratic school who, on one point, deviated from the master: he taught that money was something more than a measure and a pledge—it was an equivalent. Money had an intrinsic value, and did not depend for its validity on the royal stamp or the estimate put on it by the king.[1]

5. *Conclusion*

From Plato and Aristotle to Adam Smith, Ricardo, John Stuart Mill, and their later followers all economic treatises have had a direct or indirect relation to social ethics. The only division or difference which can be found among them concerns the ethnic or political group to which the precepts of social ethics should be applied. Some would apply them universally to the whole of mankind, while others—particularly the mercantilists—would confine them to their own respective countries at the expense of foreign lands. But the main purpose of all economic writings was to inquire what kind of economic operations would lead to the material and moral welfare of society, and what kind would result in its harm. Not the attainment of riches was their principal object, but the attainment of social justice and the prevention of social injustice, either for mankind as a whole or only—as with the mercantilists —for their own nation or country or empire.

[1] Daire, *Les Physiocrates*, pp. 886–1023.

With the economic philosophers and theologians of ancient and medieval times, this aim and end is quite manifest. Plato's *Politea* is one long discourse on the problem: "What is justice and how is it to be established?" Aristotle's economic disquisitions are comprised in his *Ethics*. No long arguments or scholastic references are necessary to support the opinion that the views of the Fathers and Doctors of the Church on trade and commerce have their roots in Christian ethics. All those philosophers and theologians considered equality of exchanges (commutative justice) the basis of all economic activities in human society.

Early modern times suffered a recession from universalism, as evidenced in the balance of trade policy, the lodestar of economic nationalism of the mercantilists, who saw in the inequality of international exchanges the main source of riches. But even they were guided by the idea of national solidarity. One of their principal writers, Lewes Roberts, introduced his tract, *Treasure of Traffike* (1641), with the words "No man is born for himself, but for the country" (p. 1), that is, no selfish interest is to be sought, but the well-being of the commonwealth.

Adam Smith, Ricardo, and their followers turned their back on mercantilism, and restored the principle of universal economic solidarity by their theoretical and practical efforts on behalf of free, reciprocal, and mutually advantageous trade among the nations of the world, thus restoring equality of exchanges or international economic justice. And it is the greatness of Quesnay and his followers that they re-erected the foundation of human solidarity, on which the British economists built. From this point of view the physiocrats deserve their title as pioneers of political economy. For in pure economic science, that is. in theories of production of commodities, in problems of value, essence of money, sources of profit, in matters of banking and finance, their contributions are necessarily negligible or non-existent. What contributions could be expected in those respects from physiocrats who, as we have learned, denied the productivity of craftsmanship and manufacture, the profitableness of trade and commerce, the equivalence of money with commodities, the legitimacy of banking and finance? Evidently none. And yet those economic categories form the largest part of modern political economy. The glory of the physiocrats rests on their social ethics, on the restoration of human solidarity, on the negation of economic nationalism, on the doctrine of equal exchanges and natural liberty, on the combination of moral discipline with economic freedom. It is those contributions which assure to them a permanent place in the history of economic thought.[1]

[1] Literature: On Quesnay and his school I have not read any book which gave more than Adam Smith's treatment of the "Agricultural System" (*Wealth of Nations*, book iv, chap. 9). I believe that my solution of "Physiocracy as a problem" is the only original attempt at an understanding of what Quesnay intended to convey. I have found only two remarks which are relevant to my interpretation of physiocracy. Loménie (*Les Mirabeau*, vol. ii, chap. 1) characterizes Quesnay's ideas as a "feudal utopia." Much more suggestive is Dr. G. Briefs (*Untersuchungen zur Klassischen National-ökonomik*, footnote, pp. 20–22), who says: "The purely economic doctrines of physiocracy may indeed be regarded as the posthumous theory of medieval economy. . . ."

INDEX

Price, equal to labour and expenses, 66, 123; in practice it is fixed by supply and demand, 122

Proudhon, French Socialist, 23; in opposition to Karl Marx, 23

Quesnay, F., 5, 6; founder of physiocracy, 13; life, 100–104; works, 106–107; against Colbert, 46, 47; economist of "Return-to-Nature," 49; influenced by Locke and Aquinas, 59, 72, 169, and by Boisguillebert, 105; on Incas and common lands, 112–113; social principles rooted in law of nature, 110–112; on inequality, 113; economic principles, 120–124; on commerce and traffic, 127–130; best policy of States, 131; conception of money, 133; against balance of trade policy, 136–137; on rate of interest, 137–138; single tax on revenue from land, 139; wages of labourers, 139–140; summary of his doctrines, 141–144; aim of physiocracy: to rationalize medieval economic life, 147; his ideal realm, 150, 167; the *Tableau*, its balance sheet, 151, 155, 158; Adam Smith on, 171–172; his service to social economics, 189

Regrating (in corn trade), 20
Rent, various definitions of, 174; according to Quesnay and Smith fertility of the soil its source, 175; "farmers

earn three rents," 174; Ricardo's theory, 175–177
"Return-to-Nature," 48–50
Ricardo, David, 173; theory of rent, 175–178; differs from Adam Smith, 176; against physiocracy, 177; corrects mercantilist view of profit, 177; theoretical representative of industrial middle class, 178

Richelieu, Cardinal, French statesman, favours mercantilist policy, 94

Roberts, Lewes, English economist (first half of seventeenth century), 58; traffic the only source of riches, 119

Rousseau, J.-J., on "return-to-nature," 50; on arts and science, 98–99, 145

St. Paul and law of nature, 54
Shakespeare, William, on Kingship, 149
St. Thomas Aquinas, on justice, 14; exchanges, 57–58; foreign trade or traffic, 58–62; agriculture, 64; just price, 66; on government, 61, 149; on tyranny, 149

Sect, meaning of, 179; contrasted with school of thought, 179

Smith, Adam, 5; admirer of Quesnay, 6; influenced by physiocracy, 73; comparison with Quesnay and Boisguillebert, 108–109; on productive and unproductive labour, 120, 124; explains rise of physiocracy ("agricultural system"), 146; impressed by Quesnay's "*œconomic table*"